William H. Behney

Choruses Adapted to Standard Hymns

A Collection for Revival Services, Prayer Meetings, etc.

William H. Behney

Choruses Adapted to Standard Hymns
A Collection for Revival Services, Prayer Meetings, etc.

ISBN/EAN: 9783337345662

Printed in Europe, USA, Canada, Australia, Japan

Cover: Foto ©Lupo / pixelio.de

More available books at **www.hansebooks.com**

CHORUSES

—ADAPTED TO—

Standard Hymns

A COL ECTION

—FOR—

Revival Services

Prayer Meetings, etc.

O come, let us sing unto the Lord. Ps. 95: 1

10 Cents per copy; $8.00 per hundred

Copyrighted by
WM. H. BEHNEY, Annville, Pa.

1

ALAS! and did my Saviour bleed?
And did my Sovereign die?
Would he devote that sacred head
For such a worm as I?

2 Was it for crimes that I have done,
He groaned upon the tree?
Amazing pity! grace unknown!
And love beyond degree!

3 Well might the sun in darkness hide,
And shut his glories in.
When Christ, the mighty Maker, died
For man, the creature's sin.

4 Thus might I hide my blushing face,
While his dear cross appears
Dissolve my heart in thankfulness,
And melt mine eyes to tears.

5 But floods of tears can ne'er repay
The debt of love I owe;
Here, Lord, I give myself away,
'Tis all that I can do.

(a) ‖ O, HOW happy we shall be when the
Lord will take us home
To rest in endless peace.

2

'TIS the promise of God, full salvation to give
Unto him who on Jesus, His son will believe.

CHO. - Hallelujah 'tis done! I believe on the Son:
I am saved by the blood of the crucified One.

2 Though the pathway be lonely and dangerous too,
  Surely Jesus is able to carry me through.

3 Many loved ones have I in yon heavenly throng.
  They are safe now in glory and this is their song.

4 Little children I see standing close by their King,
  And He smiles as their songs of salvation they sing.

5 There are prophets and kings in that throng I behold
  And they sing as they march through the streets of pure gold.

6 There's a part in that chorus for you and for me,
  And the themes of our praises forever will be :

(b) HE LOVES me, He loves me,
     He loves me this I know;
     He gave himself to die for me,
     Because He loved me so.

(c) ‖ O, WHEN I die, my soul shall fly,
     Into the arms of Jesus : ‖

3

I NEED Thee every hour,
  Most gracious Lord,
No tender voice like Thine
  Can peace afford.

Cho.—I need Thee, Oh ! I need Thee,
  Every hour I need Thee;
O bless me now my Saviour,
  I come to Thee.

2 I need Thee every hour,
   Stay Thou near by;
  Temptations lose their power
   When Thou art nigh.

3 I need Thee every hour,
   In joy or pain;
  Come quickly and abide
   Or life is in vain.

4 I need Thee every hour,
   Teach me Thy will;
  And Thy rich promises
   In me fulfill.

5 I need Thee every hour,
   Most Holy One;
  O, make me Thine indeed,
   Thou blessed Son.

(d)   PRAISE the Lord, Oh ! my soul,
       Glory, Hallelujah;
       Praise the Lord Oh ! my soul,
       Praise ye the Lord,

(e) ‖ : WE ARE building up the temple,
    Building up the temple,
    Building up the temple of the Lord : ‖

    Say, fathers will you help us,
‖ : Say, fathers will you help us : ‖
    We are building up the temple of the Lord.

    Say, mothers, &c.
    Say, brothers, &c.
    Say, sisters, &c.
    Say, children, &c.
    Say, neighbors, &c.
    All mankind should be helping,
    The Saviour surely helps us.

4

THERE is a fountain filled with blood,
  Drawn from Immanuel's veins,
And sinners plunged beneath that flood,
  Lose all their guilty stains.

2 The dying thief rejoiced to see
  That fountain in his day;
And there have I, as vile as he,
  Washed all my sins away.

3 Thou dying Lamb! thy precious blood
  Shall never lose its power,
Till all the ransomed Church of God
  Are saved to sin no more.

4 E'er since, by faith, I saw the stream
  Thy flowing wounds supply,
Redeeming love has been my theme,
  And shall be till I die.

5 Then in a nobler sweeter song,
  I'll sing Thy power to save,
When this poor lisping, stammering tongue
  Lies silent in the grave.

5

IF you from sin wish to be free,
  Oh give your heart to God;
To Jesus you will have to flee,
  Oh give your heart to God.

  CHO.—Oh! sinner, Oh! sinner,
    Give your heart to God.

2 Jesus your sin sick soul can cure,
  And from all evil make it pure.

3 "Come unto me" the Saviour says,
  And all your sins at once confess.

4 All those who ask, and do believe,
   God's blessing surely shall receive.

5 Why will you longer still delay,
   Come seek the Lord this very day.

6 As long as you in sin remain,
   Your time is surely spent in vain.

7 Though Satan wants to give you peace,
   Your wretchedness he does increase.

8 With all the pleasure that Satan gives
   He naught but you still more deceives.

9 Why will you then for Satan live,
   Who promises but can not give.

10 If you live on and die in sin,
   You cannot Heaven enter in.

11 Come, sinner, leave the world behind,
   And that rich Pearl of Beauty find.

(f)   HEAVEN is a high and holy place,
       You can't get there if you have no grace,
       It takes a regular soldier,
       To walk the Heavenly way.

(g)   ‖ WE ARE walking in the Light,
        We are walking in the Light. ‖
        We are walking in the beautiful Light of
          God.

       We have fathers in the Light.
       We have mothers, &c.
       We have brothers, &c.
       We have sisters, &c.
       We have children, &c.
       We have neighbors, &c.
       We have Jesus, &c.

6

I GAVE my life for thee,
  My precious blood I shed,
That thou mighst ramsomed be,
  And quickened from the dead,
I gave I gave my life for thee,
What hast thou given for me?

2 My Father's house of light,
  My glory-circled throne
I left for earthly night;
  For wand'rings sad and lone;
I left, I left it all for thee,
Hast thou left aught for me?

3 I suffered much for thee,
  More than thy tongue can tell,
Of bitterest agony,
  To rescue thee from hell;
I've borne, I've borne it all for thee,
What hast thou borne for me?

4 And I have brought to thee,
  Down from my home above
Salvation full and free,
  My pardon and my love;
I bring, I bring rich gifts to thee,
What hast thou brought to me?

(h) WHEN we meet, we'll shout hallelujah,
  ‖ : When we meet, we'll shout hallelujah : ‖
    In the New Jerusalem.

  We have fathers there in glory,
  ‖ : We have fathers there in glory : ‖
    In the New Jerusalem.
  By and by we'll go and see them,
  ‖ : By and by we'll go and see them : ‖
    In the New Jerusalem.

Won't that be a happy meeting,
|| : Won't that be a happy meeting, : ||
In the New Jerusalem.

We have mothers, &c.
We have brothers, &c.
We have sisters, &c.
We have children, &c.
We have angels, &c.
We have Jesus, &c.

7

I AM so glad that our Father in Heaven
Tells of His love in the Book He has given;
Wonderful things in the Bible I see;
This is the dearest that Jesus loves me.

Cho.—I am so glad that Jesus loves me,
Jesus loves me, Jesus loves me;
I am so glad that Jesus loves me,
Jesus loves even me.

2 Though I forgot him and wander away,
Still he doth love me wherever I stray;
Back to his dear loving arms would I flee,
When I remember that Jesus loves me.

3 Oh, if there's only one song I can sing,
When in His beauty I see the great King.
This shall my song in eternity be,
"Oh, what a wonder that Jesus loves me."

4 Jesus loves me, and I know I love Him,
Love brought Him down my poor soul to redeem
Yes it was love made Him die on the tree,
Oh, I am certain that Jesus loves me.

5 If one should ask of me, how could I tell?
Glory to Jesus I know very well,
God's Holy Spirit with mine doth agree,
Constantly witnessing—Jesus loves me.

6 In this assurance I find sweetest rest,
Trusting in Jesus I know I am blest;
Satan dismayed, from my soul now doth flee,·
When I just tell him that Jesus loves me

(i) ‖ : IF I only die happy . ‖
If I only die happy when I die.

Dear fathers you must watch and pray,
  If you want to die happy when you die;
And live for Jesus every day,
  If you want to die happy when you die.

Dear mothers, etc.
Dear brothers, etc.
Dear sisters, etc.
Dear children, etc.
Dear neighbors, etc.

(j) ‖ : HIGHER than I, higher than I,
Lead me to the rock that is higher than I. : ‖

(k) OH, HOW happy we shall be,
When from sin and sorrow free. [us home.
Yes happy, happy, when the Lord will call

8

IN THE resurrection morning,
  We shall see the Saviour coming,
And the sons of God a shouting,
In the kingdom of the Lord.
  Are your lamps well burning,
‖ : Are your lamps well burning, : ‖
Are your vessels filled with oil.

2 We can feel the advent glory,
While the vision seems to tarry,
And we'll comfort one another

With the Holy words of God;
  Are you free from evil,
  ‖: Are you free from evil :‖
  And unspotted from the world?

3 We are but a band of strangers
Marching through a world of dangers,
But our Saviour leads on onward,
And we'll conquer every foe :
  Then we'll join the army,
  ‖: Then we'll join the army :‖
  And defend the Saviour's cause.

4 By strong faith we can discover,
That our warfare soon is over
And we soon shall meet each other,
On bright Canaan's happy shore.
  When we cross the Jordan,
  ‖: When we cross the Jordan, :‖
  We will live to die no more.

5 O, ye saints of God take courage,
You shall soon be free from bondage,
Since dear Jesus leads the army
We shall surely gain the day.
  When we gain the victory.
  ‖: When we gain the victory, :‖
  We will lay our armor by.

6 Even though the sinful mock us,
We must carry out our mission,
And must wait for the rich promise,
Till the dawning of the day.
  We shall be delivered,
  ‖: We shall be delivered, .‖
  Who've enlisted in the war.

7 In the days of earth's dominion,
Christ has promised us a kingdom,
Which we soon shall all inherit,
And shall never be destroyed.

It shall stand forever,
‖: It shall stand forever, :‖
And we shall possess the land.

8 Let us take a shout of glory,
While declaring the sweet story,
And let us be ever ready
Our heavenly King to meet.
When we meet dear Jesus,
‖: When we meet dear Jesus, .‖
O, how happy we shall be.

9 Oh! how happy is that meeting,
When salvation is completed,
When the saints of God are shouting,
In the kingdom of the Lord.
When we meet in glory,
‖: When we meet in glory, :‖
We will shout forever more.

(1) I CAN, I will and I do believe,
‖: I can, I will and I do believe, :‖
That Jesus died for me.
He died for you, and He died for me,
‖: He died for you, and He died for me, :‖
He died for every one.

Say, fathers are you happy,
‖: Say, fathers are you happy :‖
With Jesus in the soul.
Yes, bless the Lord, 'tis happy,
‖: Yes, bless the Lord, 'tis happy, :‖
With Jesus in the soul.

Say, mothers, etc.
Say, brothers, etc.
Say, sisters, etc.
Say, children, etc.
Say, neighbors, etc.

(m) HELP ME, dear Saviour, Thee to own,
And ever faithful be;
And when Thou sittest on Thy throne,
O, Lord, remember me.

9

I WANT to go to Heaven,
And with the angels stand,
A crown upon my forehead,
A harp within my hand,
There right before my Saviour,
So glorious and so bright,
I'll sing the sweetest music,
And praise Him day and night.

2 My Saviour dear has promised,
To take me to that home
Of sweetest bliss and glory,
Forever there to roam;
To view the Heavenly beauties,
And round the Father's throne,
Rejoice, for there I never,
Have need to weep or moan.

3 I will remain a Christian,
Since Jesus promised me
If I keep firm and steadfast,
From sin He'll keep me free,
Oft will I go in prayer,
To God and ask for grace,
And labor till He calls me,
To see Him face to face.

4 Thanks be to my Redeemer,
Who gladly for me died;
Who bore my sins with meekness,
For me He was crucified;
My soul in Him rejoices,
I long each moment more,
To meet my loving Saviour
On Canaan's happy shore.

5 Fair visions of His glory,
   Go streaming through my soul;
I feel so very happy
   Since He has made me whole;
When here my work is ended,
   How soon with Him I'll be,
In that fair Heavenly Mansion,
   Through all eternity.

(n)   OH, THE blood, the precious blood,
      That Jesus shed for me !
   Upon the cross, in crimson blood,
      Just now by faith I see.

(o)   OH, DEPTH of mercy, can it be,
   The gate was left ajar for me,
   For me, for me,
   Was left ajar for me.

(p)   OH, LORD, send us a blessing,
  |: Oh, Lord, send us a blessing, :|
   Oh send us a blessing from Heaven above.

(q)   HALLELUJAH, send thy power,
      Hallelujah, amen;
   Hallelujah, send thy power,
      Revive us again.

10

COME, thou fount of every blessing,
   Tune my heart to sing Thy grace :
Streams of mercy never ceasing,
   Call for songs of loudest praise;
Teach me some melodious sonnet,
   Sung by flaming tongues above;
Praise the mount—I'm fixed upon it,
   Mount of Thy redeeming love.

2 Here I'll raise mine Ebenezer,
   Hither by Thy help I've come;
  And I hope, by Thy good pleasure,
   Safely to arrive at home.
  Jesus sought me when a stranger,
   Wand'ring from the fold of God;
  He, to rescue me from danger,
   Interpos'd His precious blood !

3 O to grace, how great a debtor,
   Daily I'm constrained to be;
  Let Thy goodness, like a fetter,
   Bind my wand'ring heart to Thee;
  Prone to wander, Lord I feel it.
   Prone to leave the God I love;
  Here's my heart, O take and seal it,
   Seal it for Thy courts above.

(r) ‖: WE'LL STAND the storm, for it won't be
   And we'll anchor by and by. :‖   [long.

(s) OH, GLORIOUS fountain, here will I stay,
   And in Thee ever wash my sins away.

(t) I DO BELIEVE, I now believe,
   That Jesus died for me,
   And through His blood, His precious blood,
   I am from sin set free.

(u) ‖: MY SOUL will overcome by the blood of
      the Lamb, :‖
   Overcome, overcome,
  Overcome by the blood of the Lamb.

(v) AT THE CROSS, at the cross, where I first
      saw the light,
   And the burden of my heart rolled away,
    It was there by faith, I received my sight
    And now I am happy all the day.

11

Pass me not, O gentle Saviour,
  Hear my humble cry;
While on others Thou art smiling,
  Do not pass me by.

Cho.—Saviour, Saviour, hear my humble cry,
  While on others Thou art calling,
  Do not pa s me by.

2 Let me at a throne of mercy
    Find a sweet relief;
  Kneeling there in deep contrition,
    Help my unbelief.

3 Trusting only in Thy merit,
    Would I seek Thy face,
  Heal my wounded, broken spirit,
    Save me by Thy grace.

4 Thou, the spring of all comfort,
    More than life to me.
  Whom have I on earth beside Thee?
  Whom in heaven but Thee?

12

What a friend we have in Jesus,
  All our sins and grief to bear;
What a privilege to carry,
  Everything to God in prayer.
Oh, what peace we often forfeit,
  Oh, what needless pain we bear—
All because we do not carry,
  Everything to God in prayer.

2 Have we trials and temptations?
    Is there trouble anywhere?
  We should never be discouraged,

Take it to the Lord in prayer.
Can we find a friend so faithful,
　Who will all our sorrows share?
Jesus knows our every weakness,
　Take it to the Lord in prayer.

3 Are we weak and heavy laden,
　　Cumbered with a load of care;
　Precious Saviour, still our refuge,
　　Take it to the Lord in prayer.
　Do thy friends despise, forsake thee?
　　Take it to the Lord in prayer;
　In His arms He'll take and shield thee
　　Thou wilt find a solace there.

(w)　LET US walk in the light,
　　　In the light, in the light,
　　Let us walk in the light,
　　　In the Light of God.

13

JESUS, keep me near the Cross,
　　There a precious fountain
Free to all—a healing stream,
　　Flows from Calvary's mountain.

　Cho.— In the Cross, in the Cross,
　　　　Be my glory ever.
　　　Till my raptured soul shall find,
　　　　Rest beyond the river.

2 Near the Cross, a trembling soul,
　　Love and mercy found me;
　There the bright and morning star,
　　Shed its beams around me.

3 Near the Cross! O Lamb of God,
　　Bring its scenes before me;
　Help me walk from day to day,
　　With it's shadows o'er me.

4 Near the Cross I'll watch and wait,
   Hoping, trusting ever,
Till I reach the golden strand,
   Just beyond the river.

14

I HEAR Thy welcome voice,
   That calls me, Lord to Thee,
For cleansing in Thy precious blood
   That flowed on Calvary.

  Cho.—I am coming, Lord !
     Coming now to Thee !
   Wash me, cleanse me in Thy blood,
     That flowed on Calvary.

2 Tho' coming weak and vile,
   Thou dost my strength assure;
Thou dost my vileness fully cleanse,
   Till spotless all and pure.

3 'Tis Jesus calls me on
   To perfect faith and love;
To perfect hope, and peace, and trust,
   For earth and heaven above.

4 'Tis Jesus who confirms
   The blessed work within,
By adding grace to welcomed grace,
   Where reigned the power of sin.

5 And He the witness gives
   To loyal hearts and free,
That every promise is fulfilled,
   If faith but brings the plea.

6 All hail, atoning blood !
   All hail, redeeming grace !
All hail, the Gift of Christ, our Lord,
   Our strength and righteousness.

(x) FILL ME now, fill me now,
Jesus come and fill me now,
Fill me with Thy hallow presence,
Come, Oh, come and fill me now.

(y) I WILL arise and go to Jesus,
He will embrace me in His arms ;
In the arms of my dear Saviour,
Oh, there are ten thousand charms.

(z) ‖: HALLELUJAH ! Hellelujah !
We are on our journey home. :‖

15

'TIS the blessed hour of prayer,
When our hearts lowly bend,
And we gather to Jesus,
Our Saviour and friend ;
If we come to Him in faith,
His protection to share,
What a balm for the weary
O how sweet to be there.

CHO.—Blessed hour of prayer,
Blessed hour of prayer,
What a balm for the weary !
O how sweet to be there.

2 'Tis the blessed hour of prayer,
When the Saviour draws near,
With a tender cempassion,
His children to hear ;
When He tells us we may cast
At His feet every care.
What a balm for the weary !
O how sweet to be there.

3 'Tis the blessed hour of prayer,
   When the tempted and tried,
  To the Saviour who loves them,
   Their sorrow confide ;
  With a sympathising heart
   He removes every care.
  What a balm for the weary !
   Oh how sweet to be there.

4 At the blessed hour of prayer,
   If we firmly believe,
  That the blessing we ask for,
   We'll surely receive.
  In the fulness of delight
   We shall lose every care ;
  What a balm for the weary !
   O how sweet to be there.

(aa)　‖: WE'LL HAVE a shout before we go,
     We'll have a shout in glory. :‖

16

HOW sweet the name of Jesus sounds,
   In a believer's ear ;
  It soothes its sorrows, heals his wounds,
   And drives away his fear.

2 It makes the wounded spirit whole,
   And calms the troubled breast ;
  'Tis manna to the hungry soul,
   And to the weary, rest.

3 Dear Name, the Rock on which I build,
   My shield and hiding place ;
  My never-failing treasure, filled
   With boundless stores of grace.

4 Jesus, my Shepherd, Saviour, Friend ;
My Prophet, Priest and King ;
My Lord, my Life, my Way, my End,—
Accept the praise I bring.

5 I would Thy boundless love proclaim
With every fleeting breath ;
So shall the music of Thy name
Refresh my soul in death.

17

THE Saviour is calling you, sinner —
Urging you now to draw nigh ;
He asks you by faith to receive Him ;
Jesus will help if you try.

CHO.—Jesus will help you, Jesus will help you,
Help you with grace from on high ;
The weakest and poorest the Saviour is call-
Jesus will help if you try.   [ing ;

2 Thro' Him there is life in believing ;
Sinner, O why will you die ?
Accept Him by faith as your Saviour,
Jesus will help if you try.

3 There's danger in longer delaying,
Swiftly the moments pass by ;
If now you will come, there is pardon,
Jesus will help if you try.

(bb) ||: I'M GLAD salvation's free :||
Salvation's free, for you and me,
I'm glad salvation's free.

18

A CHARGE to keep I have,
 A God to glorify ;
A never-dying soul to save,
 And fit it for the sky.

2 To serve the present age,
 My calling to fulfill,—
O may it all my powers engage,
 To do my Master's will.

3 Arm me with jealous care,
 As in Thy sight to live,
And O Thy servant, Lord, prepare,
 A strict account to give.

4 Help me to watch and pray
 And on Thyself rely ;
Assured, if I my trust betray,
 I shall forever die.

19

"ALMOST persuaded " now to believe,
 "Almost persuaded " Christ to receive,
Seems now some soul to say,
"Go, Spirit, go Thy way,
Some more convenient day
On Thee I'll call."

2 " Almost persuaded," come, come to-day ;
"Almost persuaded," turn not away ;
Jesus invites you here
Angels are lingering near,
Prayers rise from hearts so dear,
" O wanderer, come."

3 " Almost persuaded," harvest is past !
" Almost persuaded " doom comes at last !
" Almost " cannot avail ;
" Almost " is but to fail,
Sad sad, that bitter wail—
" Almost—but lost ! "

(cc) ‖: I KNOW He will answer my prayer ; :‖
His promise is sure, and I am secure,
I know He will answer my prayer.

(dd) HAPPY DAY, happy day,
When Jesus washed my sins away ;
He taught me how to watch and pray,
And live rejoicing every day,
Happy day, happy day,
When Jesus washed my sins away.

20

ROCK OF AGES, cleft for me
Let me hide myself in Thee ;
Let the water and the blood,
From Thy river side which flowed,
Be of sin the double cure,
Save me from its guilt and power.

2 Not the labor of my hands
Can fulfill Thy law's demands ;
Could my zeal no respite know,
Could my tears forever flow,
All for sin could not atone ;
Thou must save, and Thou alone.

3 Nothing in my hand I bring,
Simply to Thy cross I cling ;
Naked come to Thee for dress,
Helpless, look to Thee for grace ;
Foul, I to Thy Fountain fly,
Wash me Saviour, or I die.

4 While I draw this fleeting breath,
When mine eyes shall close in death,
When I soar to worlds unknown,
See Thee on the judgment throne,—
Rock of Ages, cleft for me,
Let me hide myself in Thee.

(ee) SING ON, pray on, we're gaining ground,
   Oh, glory hallelujah !
The power of God is coming down,
   Oh, glory, hallelujah.

21 BLEST be the tie that binds
   Our hearts in Christian love ;
The fellowship of kindred minds
   Is like to that above.

2 Before our Father's throne
   We pour our ardent prayers ;
Our fears, our hopes, our aims are one,
   Our comforts and our cares.

3 We share our mutual woes ;
   Our mutual burdens bear ;
And often for each other flows
   The sympathising tear.

4 When we asunder part,
   It gives us inward pain,
But we shall still be joined in heart,
   And hope to meet again.

22

JESUS, my all to heaven is gone ;
   He, whom I fix my hopes upon ;
His track I see, and I'll pursue
The narrow way till Him I view.

2 The way the holy prophets went,
The road that leads from banishment,
The King's highway of holiness,
I'll go, for all His paths are peace.

3 This is the way I long have sought,
And mourned because I found it not ;
My grief and burden long has been,
Because I was not saved from sin.

4 The more I strove against its power,
   I felt its weight and guilt the more ;
   Till late I heard my Saviour say,
   " Come hither, soul, I am the way."

5 Lo ! glad I come ; and Thou, blest Lamb,
   Shalt take me to Thee whose I am ;
   Nothing but sin have I to give,
   Nothing but love shall I receive.

6 Now will I tell to sinners round,
   What a dear Saviour I have found ;
   I'll point to Thy redeeming blood,
   And say, " Behold the way to God."

(ff) I LOVE the Lord, I know I do,
      ||: I love the Lord, I know I do, : ||
      But, best all, He loves me too.

(gg) OH, THE way is so delightful,
      In the service of the Lord ;
      Oh, the way is so delightful,
          Hallelujah !

(hh) THIS FOUNTAIN cleanses from all sin,
          And every sinner may now plunge in ;
      There's a fountain, a fountain of water and
          Ever flowing for you and for me. [blood,

(ii) I WANT TO go, I want to go,
          I want to go there too ;
      I want to go where Jesus is,
          I want to go there too.

23

JESUS, lover of my soul,
   Let me to Thy bosom fly,
While the nearer waters roll,
   While the tempest still is high ;

Hide me, O my Saviour, hide,
  Till the storm of life is past ;
Safe into the haven guide,
  O receive my soul at last.

2 Other refuge have I none ;
    Hangs my helpless soul on Thee ;
  Leave, O leave me not alone,
    Still support and comfort me.
  All my trust on Thee is stayed,
    All my help from Thee I bring,
  Cover my defenceless head,
    With the shadows of Thy wing.

3 Thou, O Christ, art all I want ;
    More than all in Thee I find ;
  Raise the fallen, cheer the faint,
    Heal the sick and lead the blind ;
  Just and holy is Thy name,
    I am all unrighteousness ;
  False and full of sin I am,
    Thou art full of truth and grace.

4 Plenteous grace with Thee is found,
    Grace to cover all my sin ;
  Let the healing streams abound,
    Make and keep me pure within ;
  Thou of life the fountain art,
    Freely let me take of Thee ;
  Spring Thou up within my heart,
    Rise to all eternity.

(jj)   O, YOU must be a lover of the Lord,
       ||: O, you must be a lover of the Lord ; ||
       Or you can't go to heaven when you die. 4

(kk) ||: OH, no ! oh, no !
       None but the righteous shall be saved. :||

(ll) ||: LORD, TAKE me as I am, :||
       O bring Thy free salvation nigh,
       And take me as I am.

24

Nearer, my God, to Thee,
  Nearer to Thee!
E'en though a cross it be
  That raiseth me;
Still all my song shall be—
  ||: Nearer, My God, to Thee, :||
    Nearer to Thee.

2 Though, like the wanderer,
    The sun gone down,
  Darkness be over me,
    My rest a stone ;
  Yet in my dreams I'd be—
    ||: Nearer, my God, to Thee, :||
      Nearer to Thee.

3 There let the way appear,
    Steps unto heaven,
  All that Thou sendest me,
    In mercy given ;
  Angels to beckon me—
    ||: Nearer, my God, to Thee, :||
      Nearer to Thee.

4 Then, with my waking thoughts,
    Bright with Thy praise,
  Out of my stony griefs,
    Bethel I'll raise ;
  So by my woes to be—
    ||: Nearer, my God, to Thee, :||
      Nearer to Thee.

5 Or, if on joyful wing,
    Cleaving the sky,
  Sun, moon and stars forgot,
    Upward I fly,
  Still all my song shall be—
    ||: Nearer, my God to Thee, :||
      Nearer to Thee.

(mm) I'VE GIVEN my heart to Jesus,
Happy am I ! Happy am I !
I've given my heart to Jesus,
Happy am I to-day !

(nn) ROCK OF Ages, cleft for me,
‖ : Rock of Ages, cleft for me, : ‖
Let me hide myself in Thee.

―――

25

JUST as I am—without one plea,
  But that Thy blood was shed for me,
And that Thou bid'st me come to Thee,
O Lamb of God, I come, I come.

2 Just as I am ; and waiting not
To rid my soul of one dark blot—
To Thee whose blood can cleanse each spot,
O Lamb of God, I come, I come.

3 Just as I am, though tossed about,
With many a conflict, many a doubt,
With fears within and foes without—
O Lamb of God, I come, I come.

4 Just as I am—poor, wretched, blind :
Sight, riches, healing of the mind
Yea all I need in Thee to find,
O Lamb of God, I come, I come.

5 Just as I am Thou wilt receive,
Wilt welcome, pardon, cleanse, relieve,
Because thy promise I believe—
O Lamb of God, I come, I come.

26

ALL my doubts I give to Jesus!
 I've His gracious promise heard—
"I shall never be confounded"
 I am trusting in that word.

Cho.—I am trusting, fully trusting,
 Sweetly trusting in His word;
I am trusting, fully trusting,
 Sweetly trusting in His word.

2 All my sin I lay on Jesus!
 He doth wash me in His blood;
He will keep me pure and holy,
 He will bring me home to God.

3 All my fears I give to Jesus!
 Rest my weary soul on him;
Tho' my way be hid in darkness,
 Never can His light grow dim.

4 All my joys I give to Jesus!
 He is all I want of bliss;
 He of all the worlds is Master,—
 He is all I need in this

5 All I am I give to Jesus!
 All my body, all my soul:
All I have, and all I hope for,
 While eternal ages roll.

27

ALL hail the power of Jesus' name!
 Let angels prostrate fall;
|: Bring forth the royal diadem,
 And crown Him—Lord of all. :|

CHORUSES.

2 Crown Him, ye martyrs of our God,
   Who from His altar call ;
‖: Extol the stem of Jesse's rod,
   And crown Him—Lord of all. :‖

3 Hail him ye heirs of David's line,
   Whom David Lord did call ;
‖: The God incarnate ! Man Divine !
   And crown Him—Lord of all. :‖

4 Ye chosen seed of Israel's race,
   Ye ransomed from the fall ;
‖: Hail Him who saves you by His grace,
   And crown Him—Lord of all. :‖

5 Sinners whose love can ne'er forget
   The wormwood and the gall ;
‖: Go, spread your trophies at His feet,
   And crown Him—Lord of all. :‖.

6 Oh, that with yonder sacred throng
   We at His feet may fall ;
‖: We'll join the everlasting song
   And crown Him—Lord of all, :‖

28

COME to Jesus, come to Jesus,
    Come to Jesus, just now ;
Just now come to Jesus,
    Come to Jesus, just now.

2 He will save you, etc.
3 He is able, etc.
4 He is willing, etc.
5 He is waiting, etc.
6 He will hear you. etc.
7 He will cleanse you, etc.
8 He'll renew you, etc.
9 He'll forgive you, etc.

CHORUSES.

10 O believe it, etc.
11 He is calling, etc.
12 Come, poor sinners, etc.
13 Come and welcome, etc.
14 Come, my neighbors, etc.
15 Get religion, etc.
16 Do not linger, etc.
17 Christ may leave you, etc.
18 Time is flying, etc.
19 Pray on, brethren, etc.

(oo) YES, JESUS loves me,
‖: Yes, Jesus loves me, :‖
The Bible tells me so.

(pp) I LINGER at the mercy seat :
Behold the Saviour, at thy feet,
Thy work in me begin, complete,
Oh, take me as I am.

(qq) I'LL LIVE for Him who died for me,
How happy then my life shall be !
I'll live for Him who died for me,
My Saviour and my God !

(rr) ‖: THERE'S A better day coming on, :‖
There's a better day, yes, a glorious day,
There's a better day coming on.

(ss) ‖: THEN PALMS of victory, crowns of
Palms of victory I shall wear. :‖   [glory

(tt) THERE'S A balm in Gilead,
To make the wounded whole ;
There's power enough in Jesus.
To heal the sin-sick soul.

(uu) Where the pearly gates shall never, never
Where the tree of life its dewy [close
shadow throws,
Where the ransomed ones in love repose,
Our glorious home shall be.

(vv) YES JESUS is mighty to save,
And all his salvation may know,
On His bosom I lean,
And His blood makes me clean,
For His blood can wash whiter than snow.

(ww) ‖: THERE WILL be no sorrow there :‖
In heaven above where all is love,
There will be no sorrow there.

(xx) WALK IN the light, walk in the light,
Walk in the light,
Walk in the light, the light of God.

29

WE speak of the realms of the blest,
That country so bright and so fair;
And oft are its glories confessed,
But what must it be to be there!

2 We speak of its freedom from sin,
From sorrow, temptation and care.
From trials without and within.
But what must it be to be there!

3 We speak of its service of love.
The robes which the glorified wear,
The church of the first—born above—
But what must it be to be there!

4 Do Thou, Lord, midst pleasure or woe,
For heaven my spirit prepare;
And shortly I also shall know,
And feel what it is to be there.

(yy) RELIGION IS the best of all,
‖: Religion is the best of all. :‖
I feel it in my soul,
Oh, there is glory, glory hallelujah,
Oh, there is glory in my soul.

(zz) WHEN THE war is over,
We shall wear a crown,
‖: We shall wear a crown :‖
And when the war is over,
We shall wear a crown
In the New Jerusalem.

30

WHEN I can read my title clear,
To mansions in the skies,
I'll bid farewell to every fear,
And wipe my weeping eyes.

2 Should earth against my soul engage,
And fiery darts be hurled,
Then I can smile at Satan's rage,
And face a frowning world.

3 Let cares like a wild deluge come,
And storms of sorrow fall,
May I but safely reach my home,
My God, my heaven, my all.

4 There shall I bathe my weary soul
In seas of heavenly rest,
And not a wave of trouble roll
Across my peaceful breast,

31

BEAUTIFUL mansions home of the blest,
    Land where the faithful, ever shall rest;
There is my treasure, there shall I be,
Lord, I am weary, lead me to Thee.

  Cho.—Saviour, be near me,
       Thy gentle voice can cheer me,
       O Jesus, my Saviour,
       Lead me to Thee.

2 Here in a desert, cheerless I roam,
Laden with sorrow, far from my home;
Clouds on my pathway, darkly I see,
Lord, I am weary, lead me to Thee.

3 Thou wilt not leave me, comfortless here,
Why should I doubt Thee, what do I fear;
Light in the distance, breaking I see,
Yet I am weary, lead me to Thee.

4 Jesus, I love Thee, dwell in my heart,
Never, O never, from me depart;
Hope like a rainbow, shining I see,
Yet I am weary, lead me to Thee.

32

GOD be with you till we meet again.
    With His counsels guide, uphold you,
With his sheep securely fold you,
God be with you till we meet again.

  Cho.—Till we meet, till we meet,
       Till we meet at Jesus' feet;
       Till we meet, till we meet,
       God be with you till we meet again.

2 God be with you till we meet again.
'Neath His wings securely hide you,
Daily manna still divide you.
God be with you till we meet again.

3 God be with you till we meet again,
When life's perils thick confound you,
Put His arms unfailing round you,
God be with you till we meet again.

4 God be with you till we meet again.
Keep love's banner floating o'er you,
Smite death's threatening wave before you,
God be with you till we meet again.

33

O WHEN shall I see Jesus,
    And dwell with Him above,
To drink the flowing fountains
    Of everlasting love?
When shall I be delivered
    From this vain world of sin,
And with my blessed Jesus
    Drink endless pleasures in.

2 But now I am a soldier,—
    My Captain's gone before,
He's given my orders,
    And tells me not to fear;
And if I held out faithful,
    A crown of life He'll give,
And all His valiant soldiers
    Eternal life shall have.

3 Through grace I am determined
    To conquer though I die,
And then away to Jesus
    On wings of love I'll fly;

Farewell to sin and sorrow,
  I bid them all adieu,
And you, my friends, prove faithful,
  And on your way pursue.

4 And if you meet with troubles
    And trials on the way,
  Then cast your care on Jesus,
    And don't forget to pray ;
  Gird on your heavenly armor
    Of faith, and hope, and love,
  And when your care is ended,
    You'll reign with him above.

5 O do not be discouraged,
    For Jesus is your friend,
  And if you lack for knowledge,
    He'll not refuse to lend ;
  Neither will He upbraid you
    Though often you request—
  He'll give you grace to conquer,
    And take you home to rest.

34

THERE'S a land that is fairer than day,
    And by faith we can see it afar.
  For the Father waits over the way,
    To prepare us a dwelling-place there.

  CHO.—In the sweet by and by,
        We shall meet on that beautiful shore,
      In the sweet by-and-by,
        We shall meet on that beautiful shore.

2 We shall sing on that beautiful shore,
    The melodious songs of the blest,
  And our spirits shall sorrow no more,
    Not a sigh for the blessing of rest.

To our bountiful Father above,
  We will offer our tribute of praise,
For the glorious gift of His love,
  And the blessings that hallow our day.

COME, we that love the Lord,
  And let our joys be known,
‖: Join in a song with sweet accord, :‖
  ‖: And thus surround the throne. :‖

CHO. — We're marching to Zion,
  Beautiful, beautiful Zion ;
  We're marching upward to Zion,
  The beautiful city of God.

Let those who refuse to sing,
  Who never knew their God ;
‖: But children of the heavenly king :‖
  ‖: May speak their joys abroad. :‖

The hill of Zion yields
  A thousand sacred sweets
‖: Before we reach the heavenly fields :‖
  ‖: Or walk the golden streets. :‖

Then let our songs abound,
  And every tear be dry ;
‖: We're marching thro' Immanuel's ground :‖
  ‖: To fairer worlds on high. :‖

MY HEAVENLY home is bright and fair,
  Nor pain, nor death can enter there ;
Its glittering powers the sun outshine,
That heavenly mansion shall be mine.

Cho.—I'm going home, I'm going home,
I'm going home to die no more,
To die no more, to die no more,
I'm going home to die no more.

2 My Father's house is built on high,
Far, far above the starry sky ;
When from this earthly prison free,
That heavenly mansion mine shall be.

3 Let others seek a home below,
Which flames devour, or waves o'erthrow,
Be mine a happier lot to own
A heavenly mansion near the throne.

4 Then fail this earth, let stars decline,
And sun and moon refuse to shine,
All nature sink and cease to be
That heavenly mansion stands for me.

37

OH, LAND of rest, for Thee I sigh,
When will the moment come,
When I shall lay my armor by,
And dwell in peace at home?

Cho.—We will wait the coming of the Lord,
||: We will wait the coming of the Lord, |}
And we'll be gathered home.

2 No tranquil joys on earth I know,
No peaceful, sheltering dome ;
This world's a wilderness of woe,
This world is not my home.

3 To Jesus Christ I sought for rest,
He bade me cease to roam ;
And fly for succor to His breast,
And He'd conduct me home.

4 Weary of wandering round and round
   This vale of sin and gloom,
 I long to leave the unhallowed ground,
   And dwell with Christ at home.

38

'TIS THE old kind religion,
   ‖: 'Tis the old kind religion, :‖
And 'tis good enough for me.

1 It was good for our fathers, etc.
2 It was good for our mothers, etc.
3 It was good for our brothers, etc.
4 It was good for our sisters, etc.
5 It was good for the praying Daniel, etc.
6 It was good for the Hebrew children, etc.
7 It was good for Paul and Silas, etc.
8 It makes soul and body happy, etc.
9 It does lead us home to heaven, etc.
10 There we'll walk and talk with Jesus, etc.

(ab) OVER THE river is an angel band,
   Over the river lies the promised land,
   There we'll walk the golden street,
   Over in the promised land.

(ac) THE Lord is here and the Lord is all around
   Jesus Christ is prepared to bless us now, [us,
   Oh, glory, and oh, glory, and oh, glory,
      The Lord is here.

(ad) ALL I want, all I want, all I want,
   Is a little more faith in Jesus.

(ae) ‖: BLESSED be the name, blessed be the
   Blessed be the name of the Lord. :‖ [name,

(af) ‖: Will you be washed,
   Washed in the blood of the Lamb. :‖

(ag) THERE IS but a narrow way my so
 traveling on,
 ‖: There is but a narrow way my soul is
 eling on,
 And my soul is on its journey home.

(ah) ‖: TO PRAISE the Lord with the ange
 To wear a starry, golden crown,
 And praise the Lord with the angels.

1 ‖: Say, fathers are you ready, :‖
 To wear a starry golden crown,
 And praise the Lord with the angels?

2 Say, mothers are you ready, etc.
3 Say, brothers are you ready, etc.
4 Say, sisters are you ready, etc.
5 Say, children are you ready, etc.
6 Say, neighbors are you ready, etc.
7 Come, sinners, come get ready, etc.
8 God calls you to get ready, etc..
9 Oh, won't we then feel happy, etc.
10 Bless God, we shall feel happy, etc.

39

ARISE my soul arise
 Shake off thy guilty fears,
The bleeding Sacrifice
 In my behalf appears;
 ‖: Before the throne my Surety stands,
 My name is written on His hands.

2 He ever lives above,
 For me to intercede,
His all redeeming love,
 His precious blood to plead;
 ‖. His blood atoned for all our race, :‖
 And sprinkles now the throne of gra

3 Five bleeding wounds he bears,
   Received on Calvary !
 They pour effectual prayers,
   They strongly speak for me;
     ‖: Forgive him, O forgive, they cry, :‖
     Nor let that ransomed sinner die !

4 The Father hears him pray,
   His dear anointed One;
 He cannot turn away,
   The presence of His Son;
     ‖: His Spirit answers to the blood, :‖
     And tells me I am born of God.

5 My God is reconciled,
   His pardoning voice I hear;
 He owns me for His child,
   I can no longer fear;
     ‖: With confidence I now draw nigh, :‖
     And Father, Abba, Father, cry.

40

I'M but a stranger here,
   Heaven is my home;
Earth is a desert drear,
   Heaven is my home;
Danger and sorrow stand
Round me on every hand;
Heaven is my Fatherland,
   Heaven is my home.

2 What though the tempest rage,
    Heaven is my home;
  Short is my pilgrimage,
    Heaven is my home;
  Time's cold and wintry blast
  Soon will be ever past,
  I shall reach home at last,
    Heaven is my home.

42   CHORUSES.

 3 There, at my Saviour's side,
  Heaven is my home;
 I shall be glorified,
  Heaven is my home;
 There are the good and blest,
 Those I love most and best,
 There too I soon found rest,
  Heaven is my home.

41

COME, ye sinners, poor and needy,
 Weak and wounded, sick and sore,
Jesus ready stands to save you,
 Full of pity, love and power :
‖: He is able, He is able,
 He is willing, doubt no more. :‖

 2 Now, ye needy, come and welcome,
  God's free bounty glorify :
 True belief and true repentance,
  Every grace that brings you nigh,
‖: Without money, without money,
  Come to Jesus Christ and buy. :‖

 3 Come, ye weary, heavy-laden,
  Bruised and mangled by the fall,
 If you tarry till you're better,
  You will never come at all;
‖: Not the righteous, not the righteous
  Sinners, Jesus came to call. :‖

 4 Agonizing in the garden,
  Your Redeemer prostrate lies !
 On the bloody tree behold Him !
  Hear Him cry before He dies :
‖: It is finished, it is finished.
  Sinners, will not this suffice ? :‖

42

IN the Christian's home in glory,
There remains a land of rest;
There my Saviour's gone before me,
To fulfill my soul's request.

Cho.—There is rest for the weary,
||: There is rest for the weary, :||
There is rest for you.
On the other side of Jordan,
In the sweet fields of Eden,
Where the tree of life is blooming,
There is rest for you.

2 He is fitting up my mansion,
Which eternally shall stand,
For my stay shall not be transient,
In that holy, happy land.

3 Death itself shall then be vanquished,
And its sting shall be withdrawn;
Shout for gladness, Oh ye ransomed,
Hail with joy this rising morn.

43

SING them over again to me,
Wonderful words of life,
Let me more of their beauty see,
Wonderful words of life.
Words of life and beauty,
Teach me faith and duty;
||: Beautiful words, wonderful words,
Wonderful words of life. :||

2 Christ, the blessed One, gives to all,
Wonderful words of life;
Sinners, list to the loving call,
Wonderful words of life.

All so freely given,
Wooing us to heaven ;
||: Beautiful words, wonderful words,
Wonderful words of life. :||

3 Sweetly echo the gospel call,
Wonderful words of life ;
Offer pardon and peace to all,
Wonderful words of life ;
Jesus, only Saviour,
Sanctify forever.
||: Beautiful words, wonderful words,
Wonderful words of life. :||

44

ON JORDAN'S stormy banks I stand,
And cast a wishful eye.
To Canaan's fair and happy land,
Where my possessions lie.

CHO.—We will rest in the fair and happy la
Just across on the evergreen shor
Sing the song of Moses and the La
By and by,
And dwell with Jesus evermore.

2 O'er all those wide-extended plains,
Shines one eternal day ;
There God the Son forever reigns,
And scatters night away.

3 When shall I reach that happy place,
And be forever blest ?
When shall I see my Father's face,
And in his bosom rest ?

4 Filled with delight, my raptured soul
Would here no longer stay ;
Tho' Jordan's waves around me roll,
Fearless I'd launch away.

45

REPEAT the story o'er and o'er,
  Of grace so full and free;
I love to hear it more and more,
  Since grace has rescued me.

Cho.—The half was never told,
  The half was never told,
  Of grace divine so wonderful,
  The half was never told.

2 Of peace I only knew the name,
  Nor found my soul its rest,
Until the sweet-voiced Angel came
  To soothe my weary breast.

3 My highest place is lying low,
  At my Redeemer's feet;
No real joy in life I know,
  But in His service sweet.

4 And oh, what rapture will it be,
  With all the host above,
To sing through all eternity
  The wonders of His love.

46

WHAT CAN wash away my sin?
  Nothing but the blood of Jesus;
What can make me whole again?
  Nothing but the blood rest of Jesus.

Cho.—O precious is the flow
  That makes me white as snow;
  No other fount I know,
  Nothing but the blood of Jesus.

2 For my cleansing this I see—
  Nothing but the blood of Jesus;
For my pardon this my plea—
  Nothing but the blood of Jesus.

3 Nothing can for sin atone—
  Nothing but the blood of Jesus;
  Naught of good that I have done—
  Nothing but the blood of Jesus.

4 This is all my hope and peace—
  Nothing but the blood of Jesus;
  This is all my righteousness—
  Nothing but the blood of Jesus

5 Glory! glory! thus I sing—
  Nothing but the blood of Jesus;
  All my praise for this I bring—
  Nothing but the blood of Jesus.

47

O LAND of rest, for thee I sigh,
  When will the moment come,
When I shall lay my armor by,
  And dwell in peace at home?

Cho.—We'll work till Jesus comes,
  ‖: We'll work till Jesus comes, :‖
  And we'll be gathered home.

2 No tranquil joys on earth I know,
  No peaceful sheltering dome,
This world's a wilderness of woe,
  This world is not my home.

3 To Jesus Christ I fled for rest;
  He bade me cease to roam;
And lean for succor on his breast,
  Till he conducts me home.

4 I sought at once my Saviour's side,
  No more my steps shall roam;
With Him I'll brave death's chilling tide
  And reach my heavenly home.

48

I SAW a way-worn traveler.
  In tattered garments clad,
And struggling up the mountain
  It seemed that he was sad;
His back was laden heavy
  His strength was almost gone,
Yet He shouted as he journeyed
  Deliverance will come.

CHO.—Then palms of victory, crowns of glory
  Palms of victory I shall wear.

2 The summer sun was shining,
  The sweat was on his brow,
His garments worn and dusty
  His step seems very slow;
But he kept pressing onward,
  For he was wending home;
Still shouting as he journeyed,
  Deliverance will come.

3 The songsters in the arbor
  That stood beside the way
Attracted his attention,
  Inviting his delay,
His watchword being "Onward!"
  He stopped his ears and ran,
Still shouting as he journeyed,
  Deliverance will come.

4 I saw him in the evening,
  The sun was bending low,
He'd overtopped the mountain,
  And reached the vale below;
And saw the golden city—
  His everlasting home—
And shouting loud, Hosanna,
  Deliverance has come!

5 While gazing on that city,
  Just on the narrow flood
A band of holy angels
  Came from the throne of God ;
They bore him on their pinions,
  Safe o'er the dazzling foam ;
And joined him in the triumph—
  Deliverance has come.

6 I heard the song of triumph
  They sang upon that shore,
Saying that Jesus has redeemed us
  To suffer nevermore ;
Then casting his eyes backward
  On the race which he had run,
He shouted loud, Hosanna!
  Deliverance has come.

49

SOWING in the morning, sowing deeds of kindness
  Sowing in the noontide and the dewy eve ;
Waiting for the harvest, and the time for reaping,
We shall come rejoicing, bringing in the sheaves.

  CHO.—||: Bringing in the sheaves, :||
    We shall come rejoicing,
    Bringing in the sheaves.

2
Sowing in the sunshine, sowing in the shadows,
Fearing neither clouds nor winter's chilling breeze,
By and by the harvest and the labor ended,
We shall come rejoicing, bringing in the sheaves.

3
Going forth with weeping, sowing for the Master,
Tho' the loss sustained, our spirit often grieves ;
When our weeping's over, He will bid us welcome,
We shall come rejoicing, bringing in the sheaves.

[AVE found a friend in Jesus, He's everything
 ?'s the fairest of ten thousand to my soul,[to me,
 Lily of the Valley, in Him alone I see
 I need to cleanse and make me fully whole.
 ɔrrow He's my comfort, in trouble He's my stay,
 :ells me every care on Him to roll.
 ʃ the Lily of the Valley, the bright and Morning
 ; the fairest of ten thousand to my soul. [Star.

.—In sorrow He's my comfort, In trouble He's
          my stay
     He tells me every care on Him to roll.
   He's the Lily of the Valley, the bright and
          Morning Star,
     He's the fairest of ten thousand to my soul.

ll my grief has taken, and all my sorrow borne,
mptations He's my strong and mighty tower ;
'e all for Him forsaken and all my idols torn
ı my heart, and now He keeps me by His power;
gh all the world forsake me, amd Satan tempt
ugh Jesus I shall safely reach the goal,[me sore
the Lily of the Valley, the bright and
          Morning Star,
the fairest of ten thousand to my soul.

ill never, never leave me, nor yet forsake me
ɛ I live by faith and do His blessed will; [here
ll of fire about me, I've nothing to fear ;
His manna He my hungry soul shall fill,
sweeping up to glory to see His blessed face,
e rivers of delight shall ever roll ;
:he Lily of the Valley, the bright and
          Morning Star ;
:he fairest of ten thousand to my soul.

4
When my warfare here is ended, I'll lay my armor down,
And go to rest in endless peace above;
There with my blessed Saviour, to wear a shining crown
Since this is possible through his great love;
Oh, must not that be happy to walk the golden street
And sing with all the ransomed and the free,
He's the Lily of the Valley, the bright and
    Morning Star,
He's the fairest of ten thousand to my soul.

51

O SAFE to the rock that is higher than I,
  My soul in its conflicts and sorrows would fly;
So sinful, so weary, Thine, Thine would I be:
Thou blest "Rock of Ages," I'm hiding in Thee,

    REF —Hiding in Thee, hiding in Thee,
        Thou blest "Rock of Ages,"
        I'm hiding in Thee.

2
In the calm of the noontide, in sorrows lone hour,
In times when temptation casts o'er me its power;
In the tempests of life, on its wide heaving sea,
Thou blest "Rock of Ages," I'm hiding in Thee.

3
How oft in the conflict, when pressed by the foe,
I have fled to my Refuge and breathed out my woe;
How often when trials like sea-billows roll,
Have I hidden in Thee, O Thou Rock of my soul.

(ai)   GLORY TO God !
        We're at the fountain drinking;
        Glory to God !
        We're on our journey home.

(aj)   OH, CANAAN, bright Canaan,
        I'm bound for the land of Canaan;
        Oh, Canaan is my happy home,
        I'm bound for the land of Canaan.

CHORUSES. 51

ak) WORTHY, worthy is the Lamb of God,
‖: Worthy, worthy is the Lamb of God :‖
That taketh away the sin of the world.

al) I'LL LINGER at the Mercy Seat,
Mercy Seat, Mercy Seat.
I'll linger at the Mercy Seat,
Where God will answer prayer.

am) ‖ : I'LL BE there, I'll be there :‖
Where the first trumpet sounds,
I'll be there.

an) ‖ : OH, LORD, God send a blessing down,
Hallelujah :‖

ao) ‖ : OVER JORDAN into glory ?
Will you go, will you go ? :‖

ap) ‖ : I FEEL like, I feel like,
I feel like shouting home. :‖

1 I love my Jesus, yes I do,
Glory hallelujah,
The fathers say they love Him,
Glory hallelujah.

2 I love my Jesus, yes I do,
The mothers say they love Him too.

3 I love my Jesus, yes I do,
The brothers say they love Him too.

4 I love my Jesus, yes I do,
The sisters say they love Him too.

5 I love my Jesus, yes I do,
The children say they love Him too.

6 I love my Jesus, yes I do,
But best of all, He loves me too.

7 Religion's good, religion's sweet,
  I found it down at Jesus' feet.
8 I tell you when I feel the best,
  When Jesus in my soul does rest.
9 When we meet Christ on yonder shore,
  We'll stay to praise Him evermore.
10 If you get there before I do,
   Lookout for me, I'm coming too.
11 If I get there before you do,
   I'll shout to see you coming too.

(aq) I'VE BEEN redeemed, I've been redeemed,
     ‖ :I've been redeemed, I've been redeemed :‖
     Been washed in the blood of the Lamb.
     Been redeemed by the blood of the Lamb,
     ‖ :Been redeemed by the blood of the Lamb :‖
     That flowed on Calvary.

(ar) PRECIOUS sunlight, precious sunlight,
     As the peaceful, happy moments roll,
     Since Jesus washed my sins away
     There is sunlight in my soul.

1 It was so dark I could not see,
  There is sunlight in my soul,
  My Saviour brought a light to me,
  There is sunlight in my soul.
2 My Saviour shook the manna tree,
  Some fell for you and some for me.
3 The more the people have to say,
  The more I'll sing, the more I'll pray.
4 I'm going to a better land,
  The home of Jesus, my best friend.
5 If you get there b-fore I do,
  Look out for me I'm coming loo.

CHORUSES. 53

6 If I get there before you do,
I'll shout to see you coming too.

(as) JESUS NOW is calling you,
Calling you calling you,
Jesus now is calling you,
Calling you to come.

(at) ‖ : SAVIOUR, WASH me in Thy blood :‖
Oh wash me in Thy blood,
And I shall be whiter than the snow.

(au) ‖ : NEARER HOME, yes, nearer home :‖
We are on our pilgrim's journey,
Jesus leads us nearer home.

(av) OH, YOU must give to God the honor,
And I must give to God the honor,
And we give Him all the honor,
In the New Jerusalem.

(aw) THIS WORLD is not my home, :‖
This world is not my resting place,
This world is not my home ;
But heaven is my home,
Heaven is my home,
Heaven is my resting place,
Yes, heaven is my home.

(ax) ‖ : HALLELUJAH, hallelujah,
So happy in the Lord, hallelujah. :‖

52

I'VE reached the land of corn and wine,
  And all its riches freely mine ;
Here shines undimmed one blissful day,
For all my night has passed away.

Cho.—O Beulah land, sweet Beulah land,
  As on the highest mount I stand,
    I look away across the sea

Where mansions are prepared for me,
And view the shining glory shore,
My heaven, my home for evermore.

2 The Saviour comes and walks with me,
And sweet communion here have we;
He gently leads me by His hand,
For this is heaven's border land.

3 A sweet perfume upon the breeze
Is borne from ever vernal trees.
And flowers that never fading grow
Where streams of life forever flow.

4 The Zephyrs seem to float to me,
Sweet sounds of heaven's melody,
As angels, with the white-robed throng,
Join in the sweet redemption song.

53

OH ! what shall I do to be saved
From the sorrows that burden my soul
Like the waves in the storm
When the winds are at war.
Chilling floods of distress o'er me roll.
What shall I do ? What shall I do ?
Oh ! what shall I do to be saved ?

2 Oh ! what shall I do to be saved,
When the pleasures of youth are all fled ?
And the friends I have loved,
From the earth are removed.
And I weep o'er the graves of the dead ?
What shall I do ? What shall I do ?
Oh ! what shall I do to be saved ?

3 Oh ! what shall I do to be saved,
When sickness my strength shall subdue ?
Or the world in a day,
Like a cloud, rolled away,
And eternity opens to view ?
What shall I do ? What shall I do ?
Oh ! what shall I do to be saved ?

4 O Lord, look in mercy on me,
Come, oh come and speak peace to my soul ;
Unto whom shall I flee,
Dearest Lord, but to Thee,
Thou can'st make my poor broken heart whole.
That will I do ! that will I do !
To Jesus I'll go and be saved.

54

DOWN at the cross where my Saviour died,
    Down, where for cleansing from sin, I cried;
There to my heart was the blood applied,
Glory to His name.

CHO.—Glory to his name, glory to his name,
    Now to my heart is the blood applied,
    Glory to His name.

2 I am so wondrously saved from sin,
Jesus so sweetly abides within ;
Here at the cross where he took me in,
Glory to His name.

3 Oh, precious fountain that saves from sin,
I am so glad I have entered in ;
Here Jesus saves me and keeps me clean,
Glory to His name.

4 Come to this fountain, so rich and sweet ;
Cast thy poor soul at the Saviour's feet ;
Plunge in to-day and be made complete ;
Glory to His name.

55

HELPLESS, I come to Jesus' blood,
    And all myself resign ;
I lose my weakness in that flood,
    And gather strength divine.

Cho.—‖ : My soul will overcome by the blood of
             the Lamb, : ‖
    Overcome, overcome,
    Overcome by the blood of the Lamb.

2 'Tis Jesus gives me life within,
    And nerves me for the fray :
  He spoiled the hosts of death and sin,
    And took their power away.

3 Though clouds of conflict hide my view,
    And foes are fierce and strong,
  Jesus name I'll struggle through,
    And enter heaven with song.

56

Lord, I care not for riches,
   Neither silver nor gold ;
I would make sure of heaven,
   I would enter the fold.
In the book of thy kingdom,
   With its pages so fair,
Tell me Jesus, my Saviour,
   Is my name written there ?

Cho.—Is my name written there,
       On the page white and fair ?
     In the book of Thy kingdom,
       Is my name written there ?

2 Lord, my sins they are many,
     Like the sands of the sea,
  But Thy blood, O my Saviour !
     Is sufficient for me ;
  For Thy promise is written
     In bright letters that glow,
  "'Tho' your sins be as scarlet,
     I will make them like snow.

3 O that beautiful city
  With its mansions of light,
With its glorified beings,
  In pure garments of white ;
Where no evil thing cometh,
  To despoil what is fair ;
Where the angels are watching,
  Yes, my name's written there.

57

HOW precious is the name !
  Brethren sing, brethren sing,
How precious is the name
  Brethren sing !
How precious is the name
  Of Christ, the Paschal Lamb,
Who bore our guilt and shame
  On the tree, on the tree,
Who bore our guilt and shame
  On the tree

2 I've given all for Christ,
  He's my all, he's my all,
I've given all for Christ,
  He's my all ;
I've given all for Christ,
  And my spirit cannot rest,
Unless He's in my breast,
  Reigning there, reigning there,
Unless He's in my breast ;
  Reigning there.

3 His easy yoke I'll bear
  With delight, with delight ;
His easy yoke I'll bear
  With delight ;
His easy yoke I'll bear,
  And His cross I will not fear.
His name I will declare
  Evermore, evermore,
His name I will declare
  Evermore.

4 And when we all get home
   We will sing, we will sing,
And when we all get home.
   We will sing.
And when we all get home,
   Around our Father's throne,
And myriads join the theme,
   We'll sing on, we'll sing on,
And myriads join the theme,
   We'll sing on.

5 Then all with the happy throng
   We'll rejoice, we'll rejoice,
Then with the happy throng
   We'll rejoice ;
Shouting glory to our King
   Till the vaults of heaven ring
And through all eternity
   We'll rejoice, we'll rejoice,
And through all eternity,
   We'll rejoice.

58

O HOW happy are they
   Who their Saviour obey,
And have laid up their treasure above !
Tongue cannot express
The sweet comfort and peace
Of a soul in its earliest love !

2 That sweet comfort was mine,
   When the favor divine
I received through the blood of the Lamb,
When my soul first believed
What a joy I received,
What a heaven in Jesus' dear name !

3 'Twas a heaven below
   My Redeemer to know,
And the angels could do nothing more
Than to fall at his feet
And the story repeat,
And the lover of sinners adore.

4 Jesus all the day long
  Was my joy and my song,
  O that all His salvation might see !
  He hath loved me I cried,
  He hath suffered and died,
  To redeem even rebels like me.

5 O the rapturous height
  Of that holy delight
  Which I felt in the life-giving blood !
  Of my Saviour possessed,
  I was perfectly blessed,
  As if filled with the fullness of God.

59

I'M glad that I was born to die ;
    From grief and woe my soul shall fly ;
  Bright angels shall convey me home,
  Away to New Jerusalem.

2 I have some friends before me gone,
  And I'm resolved to follow on ;
  They're happy round my Father's throne ;
  They're looking out for me to come.

3 I hope to meet my brethren there,
  Who used to join with me in prayer ;
  If you get there before I do,
  Look out for me, I'm coming too.

4. I'll praise my Maker while I've breath ;
  I hope to praise Him after death ;
  I hope to praise Him when I die,
  And shout salvation as I fly.

  There I shall see my glorious God
  And triumph in His blest abode ;
  My theme through all eternity,
  Shall glory, glory, glory, be.

60

THERE is a fold where none can stray,
    And pastures ever green,
Where sultry sun, or stormy day,
    Or night, is never seen.

2 Far up the everlasting hills,
    In God's own light, it lies ;
His smile its vast dimension fills
    With joy that never dies.

3 One narrow vale, one darksome wave,
    Divides that land from this ;
I have a Shepherd pledged to save,
    And bear me home to bliss.

4 Soon at His feet my soul will lie
    In life's last struggling breath,
But I shall only seem to die ;
    I shall not taste of death.

5 Far from this guilty world to be,
    Exempt from toil and strife,
To spend eternity with Thee,—
    My Saviour, this my life.

61

THERE are angels hovering round,
    There are angels hovering round,
There are angels angels hovering round.

2 To carry the tidings home.
3 To the new Jerusalem.
4 We are on our journey home.
5 Poor sinners are coming home.
6 And Jesus bids them come.
7 Let him thIt heareth, come.
8 And he that is thirsty, come.
9 And whosoever will may come.
10 There is glory all around !

62

CHILDREN of the heavenly King,
In the light, in the light,
As we journey let us sing,
In the light of God.

Cho.—Let us walk in the light,
Walk in the light,
Let us walk in the light,
In the light of God.

2 Sing our Saviour's worthy praise,
Glorious in His works and ways.

3 We are traveling home to God,
In the way our fathers trod.

4 They are happy now, and we,
Soon their happiness shall see.

5 Lift your eyes, ye sons of light,
Zion's city is in sight.

6 There our endless home shall be,
There our Lord we soon shall see.

7 Lord, obediently we'll go,
Gladly leaving all below.

8 Only Thou our leader be,
And we still will follow Thee.

63

WOULD you lose your load of sin?
Fix your eyes upon Jesus;
Would you know God's peace within?
Fix your eyes upon Jesus.

Cho.—Jesus who on the cross did die,
Jesus who lives and reigns on high,
He alone can justify,
Fix your eyes upon Jesus.

2 Would you calmly walk the wave?
Would you know his power to save?

3 Would you have your cares grow light?
Would you songs have in the night?

4 Grieving, would you comfort know?
Humble be when blessings flow.

5 Would you strength in weakness have?
See a light beyond the grave?

64

I AM waiting for Jesus to welcome me home,
To the place he has gone to prepare,
To the mansion of light and the robe pure and white
To the harp and the crown for me there.

CHO.—Waiting, waiting,
I am waiting, dear Jesus, for thee,
Ever longing,
All the beauties of heaven to see.

2
How I long to be roaming the blest fields of light,
With the dear, loving children of God,
And to sing the sweet songs as we're marching
Of redemption through Jesus' blood. [along.

3
Many loved ones have I in that beautiful land,
They are watching and waiting for me,
And they beckon me over to that bright happy
There the beauties of glory to see. [shore.

4
Roll along, then, sweet moments, and bear me away,
To my beautiful home in the sky,
To the land of the blest, where I sweely shall rest,
In the palace of Jesus on high.

65

THERE stands a holy city,
Whose age was never told,
I wandered by and heard a cry,
Within the gates of gold.

CHO.—Ho! every one that thirsteth,
Come taste the living spring,
And there be fed with living bread,
Nor heed the price you bring.

2 While thirsting, fainting, dying,
I longed to God to flee;
For life my soul was crying then,
Oh, is there life for me.

3 I ate the bread of heaven,
I drank the water free,
I left my sin, I entered in,
His blood has cleansed me.

4 Come, without price and money!
Come, buy and eat and live.
Buy richest wine, honey and milk,
All this you shall have free.

5 Oh, listen to His pleading,
While life's fair day is bright;
Lest all His calls unheeded go,
Your day be turned to night,

66 BEARING the fruit of the Spirit,
Gentleness, meekness, and love,
Thus we are following Jesus,
Up to the mansions above.
CHO.—Scattering blessings and sunshine,
Cheering the sad and the lone,
Then when the Master shall call us,
Sure of a glad welcome home.

2 Casting out all evil passions,
Envying, hatred and strife,
Walking with Jesus in spirit.
Pure in our every-day life.

3 Helping to bear other's burdens,
Heeding the law of our God;
Thus would he teach us to follow,
Pathways our dear Saviour trod.

4 Sending our prayers and our praises,
Up to our Father on high;
Sowing the seed in our weakness,
Reaping will come by and by.

INDEX.

	Page	Hymn
A charge to keep I have	22	18
Alas! and did my Saviour bleed	3	1
Almost persuaded	22	19
All my doubts I give to Jesus	29	26
All hail the power of Jesus' name	29	26
All I want	39	ad
Arise, my soul, arise	40	39
At the cross	15	v
Blest be the tie that binds	24	21
Blessed be the name	39	ae
Beautiful mansions	34	31
Bearing the fruit of the Spirit	63	66
Come, thou fount of every blessing	14	10
Come to Jesus	30	28
Come, we that love the Lord	37	35
Come, ye sinners, poor and needy	42	41
Children of the heavenly King	61	62
Down at the cross where my Sav'r died	55	54
Fill me now	19	x
Glory to God	50	ai
God be with you till we meet again	34	32
Hallelujah, send Thy power	14	q
Hallelujah, hallelujah	19	z
Happy day, happy day	23	dd
He loves me	4	b
Heaven is a high and holy place	7	f
Help me, dear Saviour, Thee to own	13	m
Helpless I come to Jesus' blood	55	55
Higher than I	10	j
How sweet the name of Jesus sounds	20	16
How precious is the name	57	57

CHORUSES.

	Page	Hymn
Hallelujah, hallelujah, so happy	53	ax
I am so glad that our Father in heav'n	9	7
I can, I will, and I do believe	12	1
I do believe, I now believe	15	t
If you from sin wish to be free	6	5
If I only die happy	10	i
I gave my life for thee	8	6
I feel like	51	ap
I hear Thy welcome voice	18	14
I have found a friend in Jesus	49	50
I know He will answer my prayer	23	cc
I linger at the mercy seat, mercy seat	31	pp
I love the Lord, I know I do	26	ff
I'll live for Him who died for me	31	qq
I'll linger at the mercy seat	51	al
I'll be there	51	am
I'm glad salvation's free	21	bb
I'm but a stranger here	41	40
I'm glad that I was born to die	59	59
I need Thee every hour	4	3
In the resurrection morning	10	8
In the Christian's home in glory	43	42
I saw a way-worn traveler	47	48
I've given my heart to Jesus	28	mm
I've reached the land of corn and wine	53	52
I want to go to heaven	13	9
I will arise and go to Jesus	19	y
I want to go	25	ii
I am waiting for Jesus	62	64
I've been redeemed	52	aq
Jesus, keep me near the cross	17	13
Jesus, my all, to heaven is gone	24	22
Jesus, lover of my soul	25	23
Just as I am, without one plea	28	25
Jesus now is calling you	53	as
Let us walk in the light	17	w
Lord, take me as I am	26	11

CHORUSES.

	Page	Hymn
Lord, I care not for riches	56	56
My soul will overcome by the blood	15	u
My heavenly home is bright and fair	37	36
Nearer, my God, to Thee	27	24
Nearer home	53	au
O, how happy we shall be	3	a
O, how happy are they	58	58
Oh, how happy we shall be	10	k
Oh, the blood, the precious blood	14	n
Oh, depths of mercy can it be	14	o
Oh, Lord, send us a blessing	14	p
Oh, glorious fountain	15	s
Oh, the way is so delightful	25	gg
Oh, you must be a lover of the Lord	26	jj
Oh, no! oh, no!	26	kk
Oh, land of rest, for Thee I sigh	38	37
Oh, Canaan, bright Canaan	50	aj
Oh, Lord God, send a blessing down	51	an
Oh! what shall I do to be saved?	54	53
Oh safe to the rock that is high'r than I	50	51
On Jordan's stormy banks I stand	44	44
Over Jordan into glory	51	ao
Over the river is an angel band	39	ab
O, when I die, my soul shall fly	4	c
O, when shall I see Jesus	35	33
O, land of rest, for thee I sigh	46	47
Oh, you must give to God the honor	53	av
Pass me not, O gentle Saviour	16	11
Praise the Lord, oh! my soul	5	d
Precious sunlight	52	ar
Religion is the best of all	33	yy
Repeat the story o'er and o'er	45	45
Rock of Ages, cleft for me	23	20
Rock of Ages, cleft for me	28	nn
Sing on, pray on	24	ee
Sing them over again to me	43	43
Sowing in the morning	48	49

CHORUSES.

	Page	Hymn
Saviour, wash me in Thy blood	53	at
There is a fountain filled with blood	6	4
The Saviour is calling you, sinner	21	17
There's a better day coming on	31	rr
There's a land that is fairer than day	36	34
There will be no sorrow there	32	ww
There's a balm in Gilead	31	tt
There is but a narrow way	40	ag
There is a fold where none can stray	60	60
Then palms of victory	31	ss
The Lord is here	39	ac
This fountain cleanses from all sin	25	hh
'Tis the promise of God	3	2
'Tis the blessed hour of prayer	19	15
'Tis the old kind religion	39	38
To praise the Lord with the angels	40	ah
There are angels hovering 'round	60	6t
Thers stands a holy city	62	65
This world is not my home	53	aw
Walk in the light	32	xx
We are building up the temple	5	c
We are walking in the light	7	g
We'll stand the storm	15	r
We'll have a shout before we go	20	aa
We speak of the realms of the blest	32	29
When we meet we'll shout hallelujah	8	h
What a friend we have in Jesus	16	12
When the war is over	33	zz
When I can read my title clear	33	30
Where the pearly gates	32	uu
What can wash away my sin?	45	46
Will you be washed?	39	af
Worthy, worthy is the Lamb of God	51	ak
Would you lose your load of sin?	61	63
Will you be washed?	39	af
Yes, Jesus is mighty to save	32	vv
Yes, Jesus loves me	31	oo

1

MEIN Gott, das hers ich bringe Dir,
 Zur gabe uud geschenk,
Du foderst dieses ja von mir,
 Des bin ich eingedenk.

2 Gib Mir, mein Kind, dein herz, spricht Du
 Das ist Mir Lieb und wert ;
Du findest anders doch nicht ruh
 Im Himmel und auf Erd'.

3 Nun Du, mein Fater, nimm es an,
 Mein Herz, veracht es nicht,
Ich geb's so gut ich's gebenn kann,
 Kehr zu mir Dein Gesicht.

4 Zwar ist est voller Suendenwust
 Und voller Eitenkeit ;
Des Guten aber unbewuzt,
 Der wahren Frommigkeit.

5 Doch aber Steht.es nun in Reu ;
 Erkennt sein'n uebelstandt,
Und traget jetzund vor Dem Schew,
 Daran's zuvor lust fand.

6 Hier fallt und liegt es Dir zu fusz
 Und schreit ; nur schlage zu ;
Zerknirsch' O Fater, dash ich busz
 Rechtschaffen vor Dir thue.

7 Zermalm mir meine hartigkeit,
 Mach murbe meinen sinn,
  Dasz ich in Seufzen, Reu und Leid
 Und Thranen ganz zerrinn.

8 Sadann nimm mich, mein Jesu Christ,
 Tauch mich tief in Dein Blut ;
Ich glaub ! dasz Du gekreuzigt bist,
 Der Welt und mir zu gut.

9 In dich wollst Du mich kleiden ein,
  Dein' unschuld ziehen an,
  Dasz ich, von allen Sunden rein,
  Vor Gott bestehen kann.

10 Hilb, das ich sei von Herzen fromm,
  Ohn' alle Heuchelei,
  Damit mein ganzei Christenthum
  Dir wohlgefallig sei.

11 Nimm gar, O Gott ! zum Tempel ein
  Mein herz hier in der zeit ;
  Ja, las es auch dein wohnhaus sein
  In jener Ewigkeit.

2

DAS neugeborne Kindelein
  Das herzliebe Jesulein ;
  Bring abermal ein neue freud,
  Der auserwahlten Christeinheit.

2 Des freuen sich die Engelein,
  Die gerne um und bei uns sein ;
  Sie singen in den luften frei,
  Dasz Gott mit uns versohnet sei.

3 Ist Gott versohnt und unser freund,
  Wass kann uns thun der arge feind,
  Trotz Teufel, Welt und Hollenfort ?
  Das Jesulein ist unser Hart.

4 Er bringt das rechte Jubeljahr,
  Was trauern wier denn immerdar ?
  Frisht auf ! jetzt ist es Singenzeit,
  Das Jesulein wend't alles Leid.

3

WAS mich auf dieser Welt betrubt,
  Das wabret kurze zeit ;
  Was aber meine, Seele liebt
  Das bleibt in Ewigkeit.

2 Drum farh, O Welt! mit Ehr' und Gelt,
  Und deiner vollust hin ;
  In Kreuz und spott kann mir mein Gott
  Erquicken herz und sinn.

3 Mein Jesus bleibet meine freund,
  Was frag'ich nach der welt?
  Welt ist nur furcht and traurigkeit,
  Die endlich selbst zerfallt.

4 Ich bin ja schon mit Gottes Sohn
  Im glauben hier vertraut,
  Der broben sitzt und hier beschutz,
  Sein' auserwahlte Braut.

5 Ach binde mich ganz festiglich,
  An dich, O Herr, mein Gott !
  So irr' ich nicht in deinem licht,
  Bis in die Lebenspfort.

4

RINGE recht, wenn Gottes Gnade
  Dich nun ziehet und bekehrt,
Das dein Geist sich recht entlade
  Von der last, die ihn beschwert.

2 Ringe, denn die pfort' ist enge
  Und der lebensweg is schmal ;
  Hier bleibt alles im gedrange
  Was nich zielt zum Himmelsaal.

3 Kampfe bis auf's blut und leben,
  Dring hinein in Gottes' Reich ;
  Will der Satan widerstreben,
  Werde weder matt, noch weich.

4 Ringe, dasz dein Eifer gluhe,
  Und die erste liebe dich
  Von der ganzen welt abziehe,
  Halbe liebe halt nicht stich.

5 Ringe mit gebet und schreien,
   Halte damit feurig an;
   Lasz dich keine zeit gereuen,
   War's auch tag und nacht gethan.

6 Hast du dann die perl errungen
   Denke ja nicht, das du nun
   Alles bose hast bezwungen,
   Das uns schaden pflegt zu thun.

7 Diesz bedenkt wohl ihr streiter,
   Streiet recht und furchtet euch
   Gehet alle tage weiter,
   Bis ihr kommt ins Himmelreich.

8 Denkt bei jedem augenblicke,
   Ob's vielleicht der letzte sei;
   Bringt die lampen ins geschicke,
   Holt stets neues Oel herbei.

5

KOMMT, ihr Suender, arm und durstig,
   Schwach und schrecklich zugericht't;
Jesu macht dar gnad' euch wurdig.
   Er verstost den Suender nicht;
‖: Er ist kraftig. Er ist machtig,
   Er ist willig, zaudert nicht. :‖

2 Nun, ihr armen, kommt wilkommen,
   Gottes friede gnade preist;
Thuet busze, glaubt von herzen,
   Busze, die von Süenden reist;
‖: Kaufs von Christo ohne preise,
   Kommt, denn Jesu niemand tauscht. :‖

3 Laszt's gewissen euch doch sagen,
   Dasz ihr noch nicht turtig seid;
Jesu hat die schuld getragen,
   Darum jetzt um gnade schreit;
‖: Gnade gibt er armen Suendern,
   Jetzstund ist die gnadenzeit. :‖

4 Kommt ihr Suender, schwer beladen,
  Durchs Gesetz zerknirscht dazu !
  Wollt ihr heilen selbst den schaden,
  Kommt ihr nimmermehr zur ruh;
  Nicht gerechten, sondern schlechten
  Suendern rufet Jesu zu.

5 Todeskampfend in dem Garten,
  Liegt der Heiland hier im thal;
  Schaut Ihn dort, erhoht am kreuze !
  Als er starb, schrie Er mit schall :
  ‖: Vollbracht ist es, vollbracht ist es !
  Ist das nicht genug fur all. :‖

6 Sehe den Gottmensch aufwarts fahren !
  Jetzt vertheidigt Er sein blut.
  Waget's auf Ihn, waget's kuhnlich,
  Scheut euch nicht, faszt frischen muth !
  ‖: Niemand anders, als nur Jesus,
  Thut hulflosen Suendern gut. :‖

7 Heil'ge Engel und die frommen
  Preise ewig Gottes Lamm;
  Ja, dort oben in dem Himmel
  Wiederhallet Jesu Nam';
  ‖: Halleluja, halleluja,
  Preiset Den, der zu uns kam. :‖

8 O wie herrlich, O wie selig,
  Ist die seel; die Gott erfreut !
  Jesu bin ich, Jesu bleib' ich,
  Durch das leiden dieser zeit.
  ‖: Halleluja, halleluja,
  Sing' ich Dir in Ewigkeit. :‖

6

ICH will streben, nach dem leben
  Wo ich selig bin.
Ich will ringen einzudringen,
Bis dasz ichs gewinn.
Halt man mich, so lauf ich fort;
Bin ich matt, so ruft das Wort :
Nur in hoffen, fortgelogen,
Bis zum Kleinod hin !

2 Als berufen zu den Stufen
  Vor des Lammes Thron,
Will ich eilen; das verweilen
Bring oft um den Lohn,
Wer auch lauft, und lauft zu schlecht,
Der versaumt sein Kronerecht.
Was dahinten, das mag schwinden,
Ich will nichts davon.

3 Jesu, richte mein gesichte
  Nur auf jene Ziel;
Lenk de schritte, stark die tritte,
Wenn ich schwachheit fuhl !
Locht die welt, so sprich mir zu;
Schimpft sie mich, so troste Du;
Dein gnade fuhr' gerade
Mich aus ihrem spiel.

4 Du muszt ziehen; mein bemuhen
  Ist zu mangelhaft.
Wo ihrs fehle, spurt die Seele;
Aber Du hast kraft,
Weil Dein blut ein leben bringt,
Und dein Geist das herz durchdringt,
Dort wirds tonen, bei dem kronen :
Gott ist's, der es schafft.

7

MEIN gemuth erfreuet sich,
Jesu, wenn ich denk' an dich ;
Mein betruebter sinn und muth,
Findet trost in deinem blut.

2 Wenn ich meinen Jesum seh'
Und in grozen sorgen steh',
So erwallet meis gemuth,
Jesulein, vor diener gut'.

3 Ruhren nicht die fogelein
Morgens ihre zungelein ;
So geschwind der tag anbrich,
Lassen sie das danken nicht.

4 Mensch, O mensch, du Ebenbild,
Ziege dich doch nicht so wild ;
Sorgest nur dein lebenlang
I'uer die kleider, speis' und trank.

5 Denke doch an jenen tag,
Da man ewig leben mag,
Mit den kleidern angethan,
Die niemand zer reiszen kann.

6 Diese kleider, solche zier,
Christus is das Hulfspanier,
So er uns aus lieb' erwarb,
Da er an dem kreuze starb.

8

WELCHE freude, welche freude wirt dort
Welche freude wird dort sein, [sein, :||
An jenem sichern ort,
Auf ewig zu loben den Herrn
||:Viele feter, viele sind schon dort, :||
Viele feter sind schon dort,
Au jonem sichern ort,
Auf ewig zu loben den Herrn.

CHORUSES. 75

2 Viele mitter, etc.
3 Viele bruder, etc.
4 Viele schwester'n, etc.
5 Viele kinder, etc.
6 Viele nochbar'n, etc.

(a) WENN ICH nur man selig sterb, :‖
 Wenn ich nur man selig sterb, weng ich sterb.

(b) ‖: WIR EILEN, wir eilen fort, kommt laszt uns weiter eilen. :‖

(c) ‖: 'S IST freude in Himmel, und ich fuehl's in meiner seel,
 Und ich lieb Gott, glori halleluja.

(d) IST NOCH ein wenig gnad, so erbarme dich
 O halle, O halle, hallelujah. [O Gott,

(e) O SEID im ernst, O seid im ernst, O halleluja,
 Wir reisen noch der Ewigkeit, O halleluja.

(f) O GOTT lasz 'runter deine kraft, halleluja. :‖

(g) DIE EHRE, die ehre, O gebt Gott die ehre

(h) WIR GEHN nach Zion, halle, O halleluja,
 Wir gehn nach New Jerusalem, halle,
 [halleluja.

(i) LIEBE, LIEBE, liebe ist der weg ;
 Dir liebe, geht zum Himmel ein,
 Durch glauben und gebet.

(j) O SEELE schwing dich in die hoh,
 Uud sag zu der welt adu ;
 O glori, O glori halleluja.

(k) ‖: O SELIG ist der gnadenstand,
 Jesus ist der weg. :‖

(l) O ALLE die ihr durstet kommet her zum
 Trinket frei und loscht den durst, [wasser
 Zions zohne and tochter.

(m) O WERD' nicht muthlos, werd' nicht
 Jesus ist der weg. [muthlos,

(n) AMEND von der reis dort kriegen wir die kron
 Kriegen wir die kron, kriegen wir die kron,
 Am end von der reis dort kriegen wir die kron,
 In New Jerusalem.

(o) ICH FUEHL so, ich fuehl so,
 Ich fuehl ich schaff mein Heil;
 Ich fuehl so, ich fuehl so,
 Ich fuehl's in meiner seel.

(p) ICH WAR so gern, ich war so gern dorthin,
 Ich war so gern wo Jesus ist,
 Ich war so gern dorthin.

(q) O, WIE wird's so herrlich sein,
 Wenn die Christen gehen heim,
 Zu bleiben ewiglich.

(r) JESUS IST noch mit uns, und er ist noch bei
 Und er sagt er will sein bei uns bis ans end.[uns,

(s) WIR GEHEN heim, wir gehen heim,
 Wir gehen heim zur ewigen ruh.

(t) ICH HOFF euch alle dort zu sehn,
 Glori Halleluja;
 Wo wir nicht mehr vonander gehn,
 Glori Halleluja.

9

HERR Jesu Christ, dich zu uns wend,
 Den heil'n Geist Du zu uns send,
Mit hilf und gnaden uns regier,
Und uns den weg zur warheit fuhr.

2 Thu auf den mund zum lobe Dein,
 Bereit das Herz zur andacht fein,
 Den glauben mehr' stark den ferstand,
 Dasz uns Dein Nam' werd wohl bekannt.

3 Bis wir singen mitt Gottes Heer,
Heilig, heilig ist Gott der Herr,
Und schauen Dich von angesicht.
In ew'ger freud und sel'gem licht.

4 Ehr sei dem Fater und dem Sohn,
Dem heil'gen Geist in einem Thron,
Der heiligen Dreieinigkeit,
Sei Lob und Preis in Ewigkeit.

10

JESU, Jesu Brunn des lebens!
Stell, ach stell dich bei uns ein,
Das wir jetzund nicht vergebens
Wirken und beisammen sein.

2 Du verheiszest ja den deinen,
Dasz du wolltest wunder thun,
Und in ihnen willst' erscheinen,
Ach! erfull's, erfull's auch nun.

3 Herr! wir tragen deinen Namen,
Herr! wir sind auf dich getauft,
Und du hast zu deinem Samen,
Uns mit deinem Blut erkauft.

4 O! so lasz uns dich erkennen,
Komm, erklare selbst dein Wort,
Das wir dich recht Meister nennen,
Und dir dienen fort und fort.

5 Bist du mitten unter denen,
Welche sich nach deinem Heil,
Mit vereintem Seufzen schnen,
O! so sei auch unser Theil.

6 Lehr' uns singen, lehr' uns beten,
Hauch uns an mit deinem Geist,
Dasz wir vor den Fater treten,
Wie es kindlich ist und heiszt.

7 Sammle die zerstreuten sinnen,
   Stor' die flatterhaftigkeit,
   Lasz uns licht und kraft gewinnen,
   Zu der Christen wesenheit.

8 O du Haupt der rechten Glieder,
   Nimm uns auch zu solchen an,
   Bring das abgewichen wieder,
   Auf die frohe Himmelsbahn.

9 Geib uns angen, gieb uns ohren,
   Geib uns herzen die der gleich;
   Mach uns redlich neugeboren,
   Herr zu deinem Himmelreich.

10 Ach! ja lehr' uns Christen werden,
   Christen, die ein licht der welt;
   Christen, die ein salz der erden :
   Ach! ja Herr, wie dir's gefallt.

11

KOMM, O komm, du Geist des Lebens,
   Wahrer Gott von Ewigkeit!
Die kraft sei nicht vergebens,
   Sie erfuellt uns jederzeit!
So wird Geist und Licht und Schein,
In den dunklen herzen sein.

2 Gib in unser herz und sinnen,
   Weisheit, Rath, Ferstandt und zucht,
Dasz wir anders nichts beginnen,
   Denn was nur dein wille sucht;
Dein erkenntnisz werde grosz,
Und mach uns vom errthum los!

3 Ziege Herr! die wahrheitstege;
   Halt uns auf der rechten bahn,
Raume boses aus dem wege,
   Schlecht und recht sei um und an;
Wirke reu an svenden statt,
Wann der fusz gestrauchelt hat,

4 Las uns stets dein zengnisz fuehlen,
   Dasz wir Gottes kinder sind,
Die auf ihn alleine zielen,
   Wann sich roth und drangsal find't;
Denn des Fater's leibesruth
Ist uns allewege gut.

5 Fuhr' uns, das wir zu ihm treten,
   Frei, mit aller freudigkeit,
Mach uns tuchtig, recht zu beten,
   Und vertritt uns allezeit :
So wird unsre bitt' erhort
Und die zuversicht gemert.

6 Wird uns auch nach troste bange,
   Dasz das herz oft rufen musz;
Ach, mein Gott! mein Gott! wie lange?
   Eich so mache den beschlusz;
Sprich der seele trostlich zu,
Und gib muth, geduld und ruh.

7 O du Geist der kraft und starke!
   Du gewisser, neuer Geist!
Fordre in uns deine werke,
   Wenn uns Satan wanken heiszt;
Schenk uns waffen in krieg,
Und erhalt in uns den sieg.

8 Herr! bewar auch unsern glauben,
   Das kein Teufel, tod noch spott,
Uns denselben mage rauben;
   Du bist unser schutz und Gott!
Sagt das fleisch gleich immer nein,
Lasz dein Wort gewisser sein.

9 Wann wir endlich sollen sterben,
   So versiehre uns jemehr,
Als des Himmelreiches Erben,
   Jener herrlichkeit und ehr;
Die uns unser Gott erkiest,
Und nicht auszuprechen ist.

(u) O BET, bet, wer beten kann,
O Halle, Halleluja,
Mein Jesus nimmt noch Sunder an,
O Halle, Halleluja

(v) 'S IST neuer muth in meiner seel
Schon herrlich auf der reise.

(w) UND ICH wart bis Jesus kommt
||: Und ich wart bis Jesus kommt, :||
Und er mich holet heim.

(x) UND ICH hab ein recht dort droben in
der himmlischen welt; [halleluja.
Und ich hab ein rech dort droben,

(y) NEIN, NEIN, O, nein,
Keine als gerechte schaun Gott.

(z) WEIT UBER dem Jordan,
Schaut das Land; schaut das Land;
Weit uber dem jordan,
Schaut's verheiszne Land.

12

ERMUNTERT euch, ihr frommen,
   Zeigt eurer lampen schien ;
Der abend ist gekommen,
   Dis finstre nacht bricht ein ;
Es hat sich aufgemachet
   Der Brautigam mit pracht :
Auf, betet, kampft und wachet,
   Bald ist est Mitternacht,

3 Macht eure lampen fertig,
   Und fuellet sie mit oel ;
Seid nun des Heils gewartig,
   Bereitet leib und seel ;
Die Wachter Zions schreien :
   Der Brautigam ist nah ;
Begegnet Ihm im reihen,
   Und singt Halleluiah.

3 Ihr klugen Jungfru'n alle,
   Hebt euer haupt empor,
   Mit Jauchzem und mit schalle,
   Zum frohen Engelschor !
   Die thur ist aufgeschlossen,
   Die hcckzeit ist bereit,
   Auf, aut, ihr Reichsgenossen,
   Der Braut'gam ist nicht weit.

4 Er wird nicht lang verziehen,
   Drum schlaft nicht wieder ein ;
   Man sicht die baume bluhen,
   Der sceone Fruhlingschein
   Verheisgt Erquickungszeiten,
   Die abendrothe zeigt,
   Den schonen tag vom weiten,
   Vor dem das dunkle weicht.

5 O Jesu, meine wonue !
   Komm bald und mach dich auf ;
   Geh auf, verlangte sonne !
   Und fordre deinen lauf.
   O Jesu, mach ein ende,
   Und fuhr' uns durch den streit !
   Wir heben haupt und hande
   Nach der erlosungszeit.

13

ACH, war' ich doch schon droben !
   Mein Heiland war ich da,
Wo dich die schaaren loben,
   Und sang' : Halleluja !
Wo wir dein antbliz schauen,
   Da sehn' ich mich hinein,
Da will ich hutten bauen
   Denn dort ist gut zu sein.

2 Da werd' ich alles sehen ;
   Den groszen schopfungsrath,
Was durch dein blut geschehen
   Und deines Geistes that.

Da feiern die gerechten,
Die ungezahlte schaar,
Mit allen deinen knechten
Das grosze Jubeljahr.

3 Mit gottlich suszen weisen
Wird mein verklarter mund,
Dich unaufhorlich preisen,
Du meines lebens grund !
Da werden meine thranen
Ein meer voll freude sein.
Ach, stille bald mein schnen,
Und hole mich hinein.

14

O WIE selig sind die
Die mit arbeit und muh'
Ihren schartz in den Himmel gelegt !
Aussprechen kann's niemand,
Was freudigkeit ich fand,
Da mein' seel' ist aus Gott neugebor'n.

2 Was vergnugen fand ich,
Da mein Jesus rief mich,
Und sein Geist mir den weg hat gezeigt !
Da ich glaubt' an sein wort,
Mir sein kraft offenbart'
Und sein blut mich von sunden befreit.

3 Es ist ein Himmel schon da,
Und mein' seel ist so froh,
Weil das Gott mein gebet hat erhort,
Die engel freuen sich
In dem Himmel ueber mich,
Desz ein suender zu Gott ist bekehrt.

4 Und den ganzen tag lang
War Jesus meinen gesang,
Fur das werk seiner gnaden in mir.
Ja, Er liebt mich ! rief ich
Ward kekreuzigt fur mich,
Zu erlosen mein' seel' schon allhier,

5 Aus dem meer seiner lieb'
Wird mein herz uberschutt't
Und die last meinen sunden war weg,
Und ich hab't nicht geglaubt,
Dasz ich konnt' sein beraubt,
Dasz ich einmal sollt' leiden darnach.

6 Und ich rief zu mein'm Gott,
Der mich frei macht aus nath,
Weil er Eli's gebet hat erhort,
Meine seel' voller muth,
Wie ein kohl'nfeuersglut,
Ganz voll liebe zu Gott, den ich ehrt.

7 O das herrliche licht
Leuchtet inwendiglich,
Das ich fuhl' in lebendiger kraft ;
Ja, gesegnet war ich,
Und der Heiland fur mich,
In der fulle der Gottheit mit macht.

8 Ach ein glucklicher stand,
Wer die gnad' hat erlangt,
Dasz mit mir warheit er singen kann so !
Ja der kann in der that
Auch enlargen die Gnad',
Dasz er leben kann heilig und froh.

9 O ! wie kostlich im schmerz,
Ist die gnade im herz,
Die erlangt wird durch Heiligungskraft,
Drum. mein seel' suchs mit muth
In des Heilandes Blut,
Das so fest wie ein'n pfeller dich macht.

15

WER will mit uns nach Zion gehn,
    Wo Christus selbst uns weide,
Wo wir um seinen Thron her stehn,
    In hochst verklarter freud' ?

2 Wo wir so manche schone schaar,
    Dort werden treffen an,
Wo sie erzahlen wunderbar,
    Was Gott fur sie gethan.

3 Ach Gott! was wird fuer freude syen,
  In jenem Land und Ort,
Da, wo kein tod, noch schmach, noch pein,
  Wird herrschen fort und fort

4 Dort liegt die guld'ne Himmels-Stadt,
  Wo alles springt und fluegt,
Die lauter guld'ne gassen hat
  Und Christus sie beleucht.

5 O schoene Stadt, O guld'ne Sonn,'
  Die dort darueben liegt,
Hab ich ja nur ein blick davon,
  Mein herz und alles fliegt.

6 Ach war ich dort, ach stund ich schon,
  Bei solcher schonen schaar,
Die dort vor Gott und seinem Thron,
  Stets schwingen sich empor.

7 Dort ist ihr kummer, noth und leid,
  Auf ewig abgewandt,
Dort tragen sie ein weiszes kleid,
  Und palmen in der hand.

8 Dort singen sie ja immerdar,
  Die schonste Melodie,
Die niemals je gasungen war,
  I'm gauzen leben hin.

(aa) ‖: LOBT BEN Herrn, lobt den Herrn,
  O meine seele. :‖

(bb) NUR GEGLAUBT, so wirst du erlost,
  ‖: Nur geglaubt, so wirst du erlost,
  Der Himmel ist dein auf ewig.

(cc) O ! DORT wird sein freude ! freude !
  Freude ! O ! dort wird sein freude !
  Wo scheidens ist nicht mehr,
  Wo scheidens ist nicht mehr,
  Von Cana'ns frohem Heer,
  Wir singen ew'gen Jubel-Ton,
  Zu Gott und auch dem Lamm.

CHORUSES.

(dd) EHRE, EHRE sei demm Lamm,
Sei dem Lamm, sei dem Lamm,
Ehre, ehre sei dem Lamm,
Im Himmel und auf erden,
Das neugeborne Kindelein,
Sie loben Gott im Himmel,
Das herzeliebe Jesulein,
Wir loben dich schon hier.

(ee) DER HERR hat mein gebet erhort,
Und seine gnade mir bescheert,
Frohe zeit, frohe zeit,
Da Jesus mich von suend befreit.

(ff) O DER weg ist so vergnuget,
In dem dienst des Herrn,
O der weg ist so vergnuget,
Halleluja.

(gg) ||: GOTT SCHENK uns neus leben,
Glori, halleluja. :||

(hh) UND ICH hab die lange zeit gewandert,
Und ich war so gern heim,
Ich sehn mich noch dem New Jerusalem.

(ii) O FREUET euch des lebens,
Balt komme eine bessre zeit,
Wart nur ein wenig.
Sie ist nicht mehr weit.

(jj) WIR GEHN nach Zion,
Halle, O halleluja,
Wir gehn nach New Jerusalem
Halle, O halleluja.

(kk) ||: JE MEHR das ich bet,
Je besser das es geht.
Und ich lieb Gott,
Glori halleluja. :||

(ll) UND O HERR, schenk mir die knade
||: Und, O Herr, schenk mir die gnade, :||
O schenk mir die gnade von Himmel her.

(mm) FAHR WOHL bruder, fahr wohl
Bis wir einander widersehn. [schwestern,

(nn) ||: HALLELUJA, halleluja,
Wird sind auf der reise heim. :||

(oo) O, HERR, gedenk an dein bitter's leiden,
Und dann gedenk an uns.

(pp) O, WEINT, weint, klagt, klagt,
Und laszt die suenden weg,
Und euch zu eurem Gott bekehrt,
Eh' dasz der Richter kommt.

(qq) ||: KOMMT ZU Jesu, kommt zu Jesu,
Er ist der euch helfen kann. :||

(rr) ||: O ZION'S Palmen, Ehrenknonen,
Kriegen wir in der Himmelische welt. :||

(ss) ICH HAB'S geglaubt und glaube es fest,
Das Jesu starb fur mich.
Und dasz ich durch Sein leiden dort,
Ewig kann selig sein.

(tt) ||: UND ICH fuehl etwas neues,
Als wie Jesus in der seel, :||
Und ich fuehl's, ich fuehl's
In meiner seel.

(uu) O KOMMT, geht mit uns,
Wir reisen nach dem Himmel,
Wo Jesus ist, wo Jesus ist,
O, kommt, geht mit uns.

(vv) MAN SIEHT die frommen gehen heim,
When Jesus rufet kommt,
Und die engel stehen fertig,
Zu begleiten wandrer heim.

(ww) BALD HAB'N wir ueberwunden,
So gehn wir in die ruh,
Anf der' andre seid dem Jordan,
Ist New Jerusalem.

(xx) WIR WANDERN nach dem grab,
Wir wandern nach dem grab mein freund,
Wir wandren nach dem grab,
Zu ruhen in der erd.

[yy) JA, ICH ring fuer den Himmel,
‖:Ja, ich ring fuer den Himmel, :‖
Wer will mit nach Zion gehn?

(zz) O, wie lieblich, wie lieblich,
Wie lieblich is Jesus,
Er ist mein Erloser,
Mein Herr und mein freund.

16

MEINE zufreidenheit;
Steht in vergnueglichkeit;
Wass ich nicht aendern kann,
Nehm ich geduldig an,
Meine zufriedenheit.

2 Seele, sei nur vergnuegt,
Wie es der Himmel fuegt:
Fallt dir schon manches schwer,
Geht's doch nicht anders her.

3 Heise dein schifflein nar,
Folge der wellen spur;
Gott ist der Steurmann,
Der es schon leiten kann.

4 Hoffnung lasz fur und fur,
Bleiben dein schiffspanier;
Sieht es heut' sturmisch drein,
Morgen wird's stiller sein.

5 Zage nicht, ob das gluck,
   Oefters dich wirft zuruck;
   Weil doch des Himmels Schlusz,
   Endlich geschehen musz.

6 Ist schon dem saamenfeld
   Manche gefahr bestellt;
   Schlagt doch der ackersmann
   Endlich die sichel an.

7 Halte geduldig still,
   Wie es Gott haben will;
   Reisz dicht durch, durch ungeduld,
   Selbst nicht aus seiner huld.

8 Geht es of wunderlich,
   Democh verzage nicht;
   Was dir dein Gott beswert,
   Bleibt dir doch uwverwehrt.

9 Wunsche nicht in der welt,
   Alles, was dir gefallt;
   Wenn es dir nutzlich war,
   Gab' dir's Gott selber her.

10 Welche Gott kinder heiszt,
   Werden oft schlecht gespeist,
   Weil Er in jener Welt,
   Ihnen ihr theil bestellt.

11 Nun dann, so halt ich still,
   Wie es der Himmel will;
   Wenn mich mein Jesus liebt,
   Macht mich kein fall betrubt

12 Jesus soll mir allein,
   Himmel und Erde sein;
   Meine zufriedeheit,
   Meine vergnuglichkeit.

17

DIE nacht der sunden ist nun fort,
  Der Herr ist meine freude!
Ach, dasz ich tausend zungen hatt',
  Um sein lob auszubreiten!

2 Micht wundert nicht, dasz Chritsen sich
    In ihrem Heiland freuen,
  Ich preis' mein' Gott mit lauter stimm',
    Und soll mich nicht gereuen.

3 Lasz Erd und Himmel frohlich sein,
    Und jauchzen hosianna;
  Denn Jesus nahm mein herze ein,
    Und speist mein' seel' mit manna!

4 Des Teufels kinder sind mir feind,
    Weil ich sing' hosianna!
  Sie wissen nicht was dieses meint,
    Dasz Gott mich speist mit manna.

5 O manna, wie bist du so susz!
    O manna, suszes manna!
  Wer eich genieszt, der singt gewisz
    Schon hier auch dort hosanna.

18

WACHT auf, ihr Christen alle,
  Es ist nun hohe zeit;
Die stimm' ruft euch mit schalle,
  Der Braut'gam ist nicht weit.
Umguertet eure lenden
  Brennt eure lampen an,
Laszt euch nicht mehr abwenden,
  Wohl von des Herren Bahn.

2 Auf, auf, und laszt uns laufen,
    Wohl durch geduld im kampf,
  Laszt uns die zeit erkanfen,
    Verschwind't sonst wie ein dampf;

Jetzt gilt es nicht mehr schlafen,
  Wer klug ist, stehet auf,
Ergreift die seelenwaffen,
  Und eilet fort im lauf.
3 Die zeiten sind gefohrlich,
  Der feind braucht groszen zorn,
Wer nicht wird kampfen ernstlich
  Wird muessen sein verlor'n;
Wer noch was lieber haben
  Wird als das ew'ge reich,
Den wird die welt begraben,
  Und sein den todten gleich.
4 Drum auf und laszt uns kampfen,
  Mit glauben stapferkeit,
Damit wir moegen dampfen,
  Die sund' und eitelkeit,
Dasz wir als ueberwinder
  Doch alle mochten gleich'
Als auserwahlte kinder,
  In unsers Vaters Reich.

19

WENN'S doch alle seelen wuszten,
  Jesu! dasz du freundlich bist;
Und der vustandt wahrer Christen
  Unaussprechlich herrlich ist'.
2 Ach, sie wurden bald mit freuden
  Aus der welt gemeinschaft gehn,
Und bei Jesu Blut und Leiden
  Fest und unbeweglich stehn'.
3 Niemand hat noch ausgegrundet,
  Ob er noch so hoch so gelehrt,
Was die seel' in Jesu findet,
  Die der welt den rucken kehrt.
4 Ewig kann sie sich erfreuen
  In dem suezen element,
Dieses wird sie nie gereuen,
  Ob sie gleich die welt verlohnt.

20

G̲IEB deinen segen diesem tag
   Zu unserm werk und that,
Damit ein jedar sagen mag,
   Wohl ! dem, der Jesum hat.

2 Wohl dem, der Jesum bei sich fuhrt,
   Schlieszt Ihn in's herz hinein;
So ist sein ganzes thun geziert,
   Und er kann selig sein.

3 Wolan, wir fangen diese zeit,
   In Jesu Namen an,
Er woll' uns geben geistesark'
   Und bess'ring von nun an.

21

W̲IE prachtig ist der Nam'?
   Brueder singt ! brueder singt !
Wie prachtig ist der Nam !
   Brueder singt
Wie prachtig ist der Nam,
   Von Christo unserm Lamm,
Der unsere suenden trug,
   An dem kreuz, an dem kreuz,
Der unsere suenden trug.
   An dem kreuz.

2 Um Christum geb' ich all's.
   Er mein all's, er mein all's,
Um Christum geb' ich alles,
   Er mein all's.
Um Christum geb ich alles,
   Und mein geist hat keine rast,
Ohn' er's in meiner brust
   Herrschend da, herrschend da;
Ohn' er's in meiner brust
   Herrschend da.

3 Sein sanftes joch ich trag'
  Mit vergnueg'n, mit vergnueg'n ;
  Sein sanftes joch ich trag
  Mit vergnueg'n.
  Sein sanftes joch ich trag',
  Sein kreuz ich fuerchte nicht,
  Sein'n Namen ich bekenn'
  Immermehr, immermehr,
  Sein'n Namen ich bekenn,
  Immermehr.

4 Ich will in seinem dienst,
  Bleiben treu, bleiben treu ;
  Ich will in seinem dienst,
  Bleiben treu.
  Ich will in seinem dienst,
  Ja, immer fahren fort,
  Wie es mich lehren thut
  Des Herrn Wort,
  Wie es mich lehren thut
  Des Herrn Wort.

5 O brueder, habt nun math,
  Es geht gut ! es geht gut !
  O brueder, habt nun muth !
  Es geht gut !
  Ei, brueder, habt doch muth ;
  Durch's kreuz dem Himmel zu !
  Dort loben wir den Herrn
  In der ruh, in der ruh ;
  Dort loben wir den Herrn,
  In der ruh.

22

JESUM nur alleine lieben,
  Der fuer mich gestorben ist,
Sich um ihn allein betrueben,
  Kannst du das mein lieber Christ ?

2 O, das bringt dir ewig wonne
  Und durchsusz' der seelen grund,
  Der geht auf die lebens sonne,
  Und erfreut dich alle stund.
3 Halleluja, last uns singen,
  Halleluja, frisch zum streit,
  Halleluja, laszt erklingen,
  Gottes Lamm in Ewigkeit.
4 Ach, wer kann den strom bescreiben,
  Der die seel mit lieb durchdringt,
  Wo mag durst und hunger bleiben,
  Da die quell im herz entspringt.
5 Niemand hat's noch ausgegrundet,
  Ob er noch so hoch gelehrt,
  Was die seel in Jesu findet,
  Die der welt den rucken kehrt.
6 Ewig kann sie sich erfreuen
  In dem sueszen element,
  Dieses wird sie nie gereuen,
  Ob sie gleich die welt verhohnt.
7 Selig kann sie sein im leben,
  Selig in der todesstuud,
  Seliges lob wird sie anheben
  Hier und dort mit vollem mund.
8 Wenn sie dort im Himmel schweben
  Auf der gulden Himmelsstrasz,
  Und mit palmen ausgezieret,
  Mit der kron auf ihrem haupt.

23

MEIN seel ist so herrlich,
  Mein herz so viel lieb,
Nun wunsch ich zu singen
  Den Engel ein lied ;
Ja singen von Jesu,
  Er hat mich erkiest
Ach dasz sie mich trugen
  Wo Jesus hin ist.

2 Mich dunkt sie herabfahren
 Zu hoeren den ton,
Vom lied' sie singen
 Vor dem gnadenthron ;
Mein Jesu zu ehren,
 Mein herz ist enflammt,
O preiset sein Namen,
 Ihr glieder allesammt.

3 O Jesu, O Jesu,
 Du salbendes Oel,
Du hast lieber Heiland,
 Geheilet mein seel,
Ach bring mich zum schauen
 Dich ewige Zier,
Dort auf jenen auen,
 Der sel'gen revier.

4 O Himmel, ach Himmel,
 Ich wnnsch zo sein da,
Bei all meinen brudern
 Dort in Gloria,
Kommt engel, ach kommt'
 Bin fertig zu gehn,
Kommt eilaud mich holt
 Und laszt mit Gott sehn.

5 Geist Gottes erhalt mich
 In Jesu ganz rein,
Und sei mein beshutzer,
 Bis er mich holt heim,
Ob wurmer hinnehmen
 Mein leib als ein raub,
Doch wird er schon scheinen,
 Obwohl er nur staub.

6 Die sonn wird verfinstert
 Der mond als wie blut,
Die erde auch brennet,
 Auf Gottes Gebot ;
Laszt blitze hinfahren,
 Wenn donner laut brullt,
Die kann mir nichts schaden,
 Der segen nur gilt.

7 Ein herrlichkeits blick'
   Erquicket mein seel,
Und singe erquickt'
   Vom freidigkeits oel ;
Mein seel da ich singe,
   Ja hupfe zu gehn,
Zum Himmel ich ringe,
   Um Jesus zu sehn.

8 Adje lieber bruder,
   Mein Jesus ruft ; komm,
Lebt wohl liebe schwestern,
   Ich reise davon ;
Die engel, die lispeln,
   Su susz in mein ohr,
Die seele wird fahren
   Zu Jesu empor.

9 Ich geh nun, nun geh ich
   Doch was musz ich sehn,
Ei Jesu in wonne,
   O lasz mich nun gehn ;
Und geh nun, nun geh ich,
   Ich geh und bin fort
O wonne, O wonne,
   O seliger ort.

(ab) O KOMMT zu eurem Jesus,
   ‖: O kommt zu eurem Jesus, :‖
   Er ist der euch erlost

(ac) UND ICH will geben Gott die ehre,
   Und do sollst geben ihm die ehre,
   Und wir geben ihm all die ehre,
   In Neu Jerusalem.

(ad) ICH WEIS eine hofnung die Gott Giebt,
   Eine hofnung die ist mein ;
   Ein hofnung wan die welt verghet,
   Sie fierd zum Himmel ein.

(ae) 'S IST ein beser'n tag am kommen,
Herlischer werd's in Himmel sein;
's ist ein beser'n tag am komer,
Die ewighe ruh.

(af) SINGT HALLELUJA! singt halleluja!
Singt glori! singt halle,
Singt halleluja.

(ag) WAS FUHL ich so froh das Jesus lieb mich,
Das Jesus liebt mich, Jesus liebt mich,
Was fuhl ich so froh, das Jesus liebt mich,
Jesus liebt mich, ja mich.

(ah) LEBEN WIR in gerechtigkeit,
So storben wir in zufriedenheit,
Wann ich starb so ererb ich die seligkeit.

(ai) O JERUSALEM du schohne Stadt,
Wann zieg ich zu dir ein;
Wo die fruhling's wenden wahen,
Und dort ist' gut zu sein.

(aj) ICH VERTRAUE, ich vertraue,
Ich vertraue in seim Wort;
Ich vertraue, ich vertraue,
Ich vertraue in seim Wort.

(ak) LAST UNS wandel'n in dem licht,
In dem licht, in dem licht.
Last uns wandel'n in dem licht,
In dem licht des Herrn.

(al) EIN FELIGHES heil, ein felighes heil,
In Christo, in Jesu, ein felighes heil.

(am) 'S IST ein Brunnen, ein Brunnen
Von Wasser und blut,
Und er fleszet fur mich und fur dich,
Er ist fur alle, grohs und klein,
Und er macht von alle sunden rein,
's ist ein Brunnen, ein Brunnen
Von wasser und blut,
Und er fleszet fur mich und dich.

(an) ‖: MEI SEELE uberwind durch des Lamm's blut, :‖
Uberwind uberwind, uberwind durch des Lamm's blut.

(ao) HALLELUJA! IMMER weider; halleluja, Halleluja! immer weider, [amen.
Bis wir gehn in's Canaan.

(ap) ‖: IN DER susz Himmel's ru h,
Dort dreffen wir einander ahn, :‖

(aq) WIR KOM'N immer negher, negher,
Wir kom'n immer negher,
Zur Himmelischen ruh.

(ar) ‖: DIE HAELFT war nie gesacht.
Von Christi blut, so wunderbarh,
Die haelft war nie gesacht.

(as) AMEN, AMEN, mein Jesus is am kom'n,
O halle, O halle, halleluja!

(at) JA WIR kom'n in den Himmel,
Den schohnen, schohen Himmel,
Ja wir kom'n in den Himmel,
Wen wir drei sein bis an's end,

(au) GEHET MIT, gehet mit,
Gehet den ganzen weg mit furt;
Gehet mit, gehet mit,
Zu schauen d is liebe Lamm.

(av) AN DEM kreuz, an dem kreuz,
Will ich mich verknugen,
Bis mi seele ruhe find,
Uber dem Jordan druben.

(aw) ‖: Jesu Nam, O wie susz,
Freud im Himmel und auf erd'. :‖

(ax) KOMM ARMER sunder, verlasze die welt.
Komm und erlange vergebung der sund,
Durch buse, und glaube wi's Jesu befehlt
Jesus dein Heiland ruft komm.

(ay) Ich gab mein herz zu Jesus,
 Herlich fuhl ich, herlich fuhl ich,
 Ich gab mein herz zu Jesus,
 Herlich ist meine seel'.

(az) JA JESUS liebt mich,
 ‖:Ja, Jesus liebt mich, :‖
 Die Biebel sagt mir so.

(ba) KOMM ARMER sinder verlasze die welt,
 Komm und erlange vergabuug der sind ;
 Durich buse und glaube bis Jesus gefelt,
 Jesus dein heiland ruft komm.

(be) Heilich, heilich ist der Herr,
 ‖: Heilich, heilich ist der Herr :‖
 Gelobet sei sein namn.

(bi) Heil, heil, heil ich habs gefunde,
 Jesu meinen besten freund,
 Durich verfolge, hohn und spott,
 Will ich dienen meinem Gott, [zu.
 Und wir gehn mit freude noch dem Himmel

24

DORT ist ein Vaterland,
 Weit, hoch und schon,
Wo alle heiligen
 In klarheit stehn,
Wo alles leiden end't,
Und die freud kein ende nimmt,
Und jede harfe klingt halleluja.

2 Kommt zu dem freudensaal,
 Kommt, kommt mit uns,
Hier in dem thranenthal
 Hofft ihr umsonst ;
Dort werd't ihr selig sein,
Vor der sund und trubsal rein
Und mit dem Brautigam ewig vereint.

3 Dort in der Gottes Stadt,
   Wo lust und freund
 Niemals ein ende hat,
   Sind sie vereint
 Mitt Gott, dem friedensfurst.
 Unserm Heiland Jesus Christ,
 Und allen Heiligen in Ewigkeit.

4 O welche freud and wonn,
   Selige Braut,
 Das wir hienieden schon
   Mit ihr vertraut.
 Und ist wie Paulus schreibt,
 Dasz das leiden dieser zeit
 Nicht werth der herrlichkeit fur uns bereit.

5 O warum zaudert ihr,
   Macht euch doch auf,
 Weil bald der zeiger hier
   End't seinen lauf,
 Nach dieser gnadenzeit,
 Folgt die lange ewigkeit,
 Macht euch in eil bereit, folgt Jesu Lehr.

6 Die euch den schmalen weg
   Zum Himmel fuhrt,
 Wo euch das Hochzeitsklied
   Ewiglich ziert
 Kronen und Palmenzweig,
 Tragen sie in jenem Reich,
 Und Sind dem Lamm dortgleich in ewigkeit.

7 Damn werd ich selig sein,
   In jener welt,
 Wo keinen trubsal mehr
   Euch dort anfallt,
 Mit der auserwahlten schaar,
 Welche schon Johannes sah
 Singen Viktoria, Halleluja.

25

K OMMT bruder, kommt, wir eilen fort,
  Nach Neu Jerusalem;
Vermerkt ihr nich die guldne pfort,
  Die dorten vor eich glimmt?

2 Stracks eure augen wendet hin,
    Folgt Jesus treuer lehr';
  Halt Wachen betet in dem sinn,
    So fall die reis' nicht schwer.

3 Hier ist ein groszt wildernisz,
    Da mussen wir noch durch;
  Da schmeckt des Himmels Manna susz,
    Ach werd't nur nicht murrisch.

4 Bald landen wir am Jordan an,
    Der an des Stadt hin lauft:
  Wer glauben halt, daruber kann,
    Das wisser selbst ihm weicht.

5 Wir stimmen Moses Lobesang
    Auf Jordans Ufer an,
  Und auch des Lammes Triumphlied
    Im suszen Jubelton.

6 Dort leigt die gold'ne Himmelstadt,
    Da alles springt und fleucht,
  Die lauter gold'ne Straszen hat,
    Und Christus sie beleucht.

7 O schonste stadt! O gold ne sonn,
    Die dort daruber liegt!
  Hab' ich ja nur ein'n blick davon,
    Mein herz und alles fliegt.

8 Ach war ich dort! ach, stundt ich schon
    Bei solcher schonen schaar,
  Die dort vor Gott und scinem Thron
    Stets schwinget sich empor!

www.ingramcontent.com/pod-product-compliance
Lightning Source LLC
Chambersburg PA
CBHW020858160426
43192CB00007B/978